PICKUP SUM 1984

MICHIGAN STATE UNIVERSITY
LIBRARY

NOV 01 2017

WITHDRAWN

D1355771

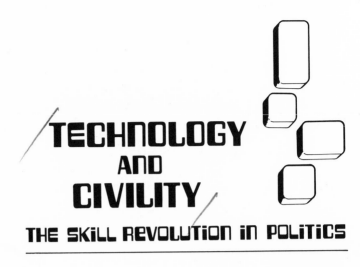

TECHNOLOGY
AND
CIVILITY
THE SKILL REVOLUTION IN POLITICS

HEINZ EULAU

HOOVER INSTITUTION PRESS

Stanford University   Stanford, California 94305

The Hoover Institution on War, Revolution and Peace, founded at Stanford University in 1919 by the late President Herbert Hoover, is a center for advanced study and research on public and international affairs in the twentieth century. The views expressed in its publications are entirely those of the authors and do not necessarily reflect the views of the staff, officers, or Board of Overseers of the Hoover Institution.

JA
74
.E884

Hoover Institution Publication 167

© 1977 by the Board of Trustees of the
Leland Stanford Junior University
All rights reserved

International Standard Book Number: 0-8179-6671-4
Library of Congress Catalog Card Number: 76-48483
Printed in the United States of America

To Cleo
Skill Specialist in Human Relations

CONTENTS

ACKNOWLEDGMENTS

Chapter 1, "Com-Com Technology and Political Behavior," a previously unpublished address to the annual meeting of official representatives of the Inter-University Consortium for Political Research, Ann Arbor, Michigan, October 22, 1971, is reprinted here by permission of the Dunellen Publishing Company.

Chapter 2, "Potential Effects of the Information Utility," prepared for a conference on "Information Utilities and Social Choice," held at the University of Chicago, December 2–3, 1969, is reprinted with permission of the publisher, from Harold Sackman and Norman Nie, eds., *The Information Utility and Social Choice* (Montvale, N.J.: American Federation of Information Processing Societies Press, 1970), pp. 187–99.

Chapter 3, "Technology and the Fear of Civility," originally presented before the annual meeting of the Southern Political Science Association in Gatlinburg, Tennessee, November 12, 1971, is reprinted, with permission of the publisher, from *The Journal of Politics* 35 (May 1973): 367–85.

Chapter 4, "Politics and Education: The Long View and the Short," which opened discussion of a research workshop on the politics of education, held at Stanford University, September 14–16, 1970, under the sponsorship of the Committee on Basic Research in Education of the National Research Council's former Division of Behavioral Sciences, is reprinted, with permission of the publisher, from Michael W. Kirst, ed., *State, School, and Politics: Research Directions* (Lexington, Mass.: D. C. Heath and Company, 1972), pp. 1–9.

Chapter 5, "Political Norms in Educational Policy Making," presented before the annual meeting of the American Council on Education in St. Louis, Missouri, October 8, 1970, is reprinted, with permission of the publisher, from W. Todd Furniss, ed., *Higher Education for Everybody?* (Washington, D.C.: American Council on Education, 1971), pp. 207–23.

Chapter 6, "Reason and Relevance: On a Madness of Recent Times," presented before the annual meeting of the Midwest Political Science Association in Chicago, April 28, 1972, is reprinted with permission from October 1972 *Student Lawyer,* the magazine of the Law Student Division; © 1972 American Bar Association; pp. 16–19, 62–63, 68.

Chapter 7, "Skill Revolution and Consultative Commonwealth," the presidential address delivered at the annual meeting of the American Political Science Association, Washington, D.C., September 7, 1972, is reprinted, with permission of the publisher, from *The American Political Science Review* 76 (March 1973): 169−91.

INTRODUCTION

A fascinating intellectual problem facing the political historian as participant observer of the contemporary scene is the relationship between long-term secular trends moving in one direction and short-term events pointing in another. Yet, the problem may be a pseudo problem. In our time, current trends and events are described, fashionably, by the prefixes "post" and "counter," and one hears a good deal about "post-industrial society" and "counter-culture" (or, as in my own field of political science, about a "post-behavioral revolution" which, it turns out, is more "counter" than "post," and which has succumbed to sudden death). It should be clear that I am not impressed by the prophetic voices of the kind one heard in the early seventies, in this country and abroad.

Nevertheless, these voices penetrated the groves of academe and forced themselves to our attention. Those were years of turmoil for universities and learned associations alike, from which there was little chance of escape. Those of us who found ourselves in positions of professional leadership had some obligation to respond, even though such action sometimes violated, as in my own case, a cherished sense of scholarly privacy. I personally had taken on a number of administrative responsibilities within the university as well as a number of organizational commitments outside it that exposed me to the tensions and conflicts of the period. All of the chapters in this volume were originally addresses or lectures given before professional audiences between 1970 and 1972. Lecturing gave me an opportunity to respond to those who, it seemed to me, were challenging the scholarly and scientific integrity of the university. If these papers are at times something less than objective, it is because I came to appreciate Edmund Burke's dictum that "the only thing necessary for the triumph of evil is for good men to do nothing."

It seemed to me then, and it seems to me now, that the scientific approach to the understanding of human affairs and, in the long run, to the solving of social problems is equally threatened by the enthusiastic advocates of the "technological fix" and by the cheerful apostles of a "greening community." Both speak in the name of a democracy that never was and never will be. The push-button democrats of a technology-dominated future seem to be as opposed to representative government as are the participatory democrats of the counter-culture. If the com-com engineers do not propose to vote with their feet as the counter-culturists recommend, it is due more to good etiquette than to conviction.

"Com-Com Technology and Political Behavior" (Chapter 1) distinguishes, therefore, between a responsible orientation toward the future and an ill-conceived futurism of ideologues who see in the new computer-communication technology only "good" or "bad," depending on personal predispositions quite unrelated to what is empirically known about political behavior. A responsible future-oriented, but not futuristic, social science can deal in "developmental constructs" that serve to give direction to empirical research in the present, but it cannot afford to be prophetic. Unlike the futurism, characterized by what I call the "unless syndrome," that makes predictions into self-fulfilling or self-denying prophecies, a responsibly future-oriented social science, rather than ignoring past and present, builds on the continuity of past, present, *and* future. Such a social science assesses the potentialities for political behavior of the new technologies in terms of what is known about politics, on the one hand, and in terms of the reverse effects of political behavior on the new technologies, on the other. While the results of interactions between the com-com technology and a country's political propensities will undoubtedly have some effect on the operation of representative government, this effect is likely to be neither as benign nor as catastrophic as futurists of either right or left want us to believe.

The theme of likely citizen response to com-com technology is more directly treated in "Potential Effects of the Information Utility" (Chapter 2). Although push-button democracy is technologically feasible, it is improbable that the ordinary citizen will make more use of it than he does of today's ballot—for the simple reason that the new technology will increase rather than reduce information costs. Judging from all we know about political behavior, it is clear that citizens are not presently willing to exert themselves in the manner that models of rational action assume (and, for *theoretical* reasons, must assume). Insofar as the proper use of com-com technology would require citizens to become infinitely better informed about public issues than they are now, the interactive utility will not have the real-world political consequences envisaged by the more enthusiastic communication engineers.

The simplistic view of democracy shared by technologists and anti-technologists is more fully treated in "Technology and the Fear of Civility" (Chapter 3). My argument is that their democratic protestations notwithstanding, the technological and anti-technological futurists share a mutual distrust of the democratic and civil politics that fail to reinforce their utopian aspirations. A politics of civility proceeds from the simple assumptions that one cannot have everything one wants, as the small child desires, and that tolerance and compromise are the mature person's responses to the existence of interpersonal constraints and environmental limitations. The conclusion one reaches is that the post-industrial technologists and the counter-culturists have more in common than meets the eye. Fortunately, neither position is likely to defy the common laws of governance which, I suspect are more robust than the prophecies of things to come.

Whatever the outcome, futurisms of all kinds are inimical to the educational enterprise because they substitute fancy for fact, teleology for theory, and mystery for method. Persons victimized by siren songs of the new saviors—technological, counter-cultural, or, more recently, pseudo-religious—are not "educable" in any meaningful sense. To what extent the university as the central institution dedicated to learning can tolerate this situation, or is permitted to tolerate it, is a question of great concern. If the question is not to be answered by power politics, as I think it should not, it must then be answered only by those who are involved in effective, pragmatic educational decision making, inside and outside the academic community. It is certainly not surprising that speculation concerning the relationship between education and politics has always been of great interest, from the Greek philosophers down to the present. "Politics and Education: The Long View and the Short" (Chapter 4) reviews some past ideas and suggests some questions to be answered by research.

Academicians and philosophers, however, are not the only parties interested in the politics of education. There are also the politicians upon whose goodwill and support the educational enterprise ultimately depends. "Political Norms in Educational Policy Making" (Chapter 5), based on information from interviews with knowledgeable legislators in nine American states, presents some of the criteria of choice that guide these elected officials as public custodians of the educational enterprise. That their concerns and approaches to educational decision making deserve close attention, even if one disagrees with them, would seem to make pragmatic sense; but such sense does not always guide all constituents of the educational estate.

A pragmatic approach in educational policy is least likely to guide the students who increasingly seek to participate in university decision making. There is some risk in treating the early seventies as typical or prototypical, for too many issues all at once inspired the demand for "relevance" that had its own peculiar meaning in those years. As I look back on the events that occasioned "Reason and Relevance: On a Madness of Recent Times" (Chapter 6), I am still flabbergasted as to how they could have happened. The issue is not that the students reacted negatively to the troubles of the times—the war in Vietnam, the plight of the underprivileged, or the abuse of the natural environment. The issue is why the various protest movements took the anti-intellectual and intolerant forms they did. Protest as a means of petitioning rulers is as democratic as cheesecake is said to be American, but student protest behavior went beyond rational conduct. "Doing your thing" became the principal guide to behavior, regardless of intentions or consequences. Only the a-historical conscience can assume that everything is related to everything else in some mysterious way. Innocent of the past and vague about the future, the student movement assumed causes and effects that were freed of the laws of causation.

It was in this intellectual atmosphere—of technological futurism, counter-cultural utopianism, and student rebellion—that I prepared "Skill Revolution and Consultative Commonwealth" (Chapter 7). If the previous chapters are critical and polemical, this last chapter is self-consciously scholarly, dispassionate, and disinterested. It is concerned with the future; it shows respect for the past; it is aware of present conditions; it deals with trends; it is stated in terms of proba-bility; and it is based on a large body of theory and research. The chapter presents a developmental construct, called "consultative commonwealth," which sug-gests that the future society will require skill and technology as necessary condi-tions of the good life, but that the traditional norms and rules of a free society will be equally necessary.

"Skill politics" is the critical variable in the emergent commonwealth of the last quarter of the twentieth century. Political modernity means that skill (spe-cialized knowledge, expertise) has replaced most other criteria for judging the capacity of elites to govern. Skill has replaced class and status as sufficient conditions for political advancement and rulership, regardless of whether the mode of recruitment into governing positions is electoral or bureaucratic.

Skill is to the individual person what technology is to society. A society's technological developments in politically sensitive fields such as communication, computation, and education are accompanied by, if not predicated on, corre-sponding individual-level developments in a great number of politically relevant skills. Nevertheless, the technologically induced revolution in skills may come into conflict with traditional, and especially with democratic or representational, ways of elite recruitment and elite behavior. That these conflicts are soluble without the necessity of destroying either the new technology or the old politics is the burden of the argument.

Whether or not one sees technology and politics in conflict depends on one's attitude toward technology and also on one's conception of what politics is about. Alternative models of democracy, such as the participatory, the competitive, or the representational, and different models of the territorial allocation of authority are likely to make for different expectations concerning the skills that political elites should bring to the tasks of governance. The notion that skill elites are not detrimental to the functioning of a free society, but indeed desirable, has yet to be absorbed into a theory of democracy that satisfies the conditions imposed on politics by a high level of technology.

1 COM-COM TECHNOLOGY AND POLITICAL BEHAVIOR

There is much speculation and little research on the impact of technological innovations on society or the political consequences of this impact. The question to be initially asked is, What makes for the helplessness of empirical research when it confronts the future? The question begets the answer: empirical research is not sufficiently future-oriented. While it is a commonplace to say that social science research is contextual, the context referred to is only the present or recent past. This is largely due to the emphasis on valid and reliable knowledge that makes social scientists shy away from locating their research in a frame of reference envisaging the future. In that respect social scientists are as rootless as the futurists; just as the futurists ignore empirical knowledge about the present, so social scientists ignore alternative constructs of the future that might give direction to their research.

A case in point is the potential effect of new developments in the computer and communication technology on politics. There is almost no research that would shed empirical light on the prospects before us. Instead, review of the literature suggests, there is an abundance of ax grinding, bellyaching, and self-serving speculation. This speculation would hardly deserve attention, were it not for the fact that it defines and molds the intellectual climate, especially as conveyed through the mass media, in which both public decision-makers and the attentive public orient themselves to the future. As one reads what futurists have to say, regardless of whether they are members of the establishment, so called, or of the counter-culture, so called, the impression is one of collective confusion. An incredible mass of nonsense is being spawned about the political impact of the computer and communication technologies. There was a time, in the years immediately before and after the Second World War, when propaganda analysis was an honorable pursuit in social science. This kind of study has been neglected in recent years; it deserves being revived. For ideological warfare threatens serious inquiry into the implications of the computer and communication technologies for politics and public policy. Social science cannot flourish and do its job in such an intellectual atmosphere. The needs of both public policy and social science require that ideological presuppositions about the implications of the computer and communication technologies for social and political life be unmasked.

There are four areas of concern about the socio-political implications of what will be called the "com-com technology." First, there are implications for civil liberties and the protection of privacy. Here some fine work has been done and is being done by a few social scientists. Second, there are implications of the com-com technology for administrative decision-making. The writing here is considerable and reasonably balanced because computers and communication linkages are already used as extensions of previously manual information systems, so that there is an experiential base for anticipating future developments.[3] There are problems, however, because these developments are tied up, in turn, with the unknown future of such social-engineering or procedurally rational strategies as programming-planning-budgeting, operations research, and systems analysis generally. Scholars in public law and administration will attend to these matters and through their research enlighten the main stream of political science. Third, there are implications of the com-com technology for public policy more generally—implications that involve the establishment of massive data banks and the creation of social indicators. The controversies surrounding the suggestion for a National Data Center, some years ago, and the difficulties facing what is sometimes called the "social indicator movement" are familiar.

There is a fourth area of concern—the implications of the com-com technology for political behavior or, in the grand perspective, for representative government. This is the area where political science is mot immediately involved and where research on political behavior and political processes can make an immediate contribution. Political science has produced, in the last fifteen years or so, an impressive body of empirical research and much reliable knowledge on political behavior. But this knowledge is contextual in the present. Few political scientists have given much attention to its relevance for the future or conducted their research in a frame of reference that includes the future as a parameter. There is, of course, good reason for this—empirical researchers are not inclined to prophecy.

There is now a voluminous literature on technology and the presumed impact of technology on all kinds of things—the environment, population, war and peace, leisure, social structure and social change, and even politics. Insofar as these writings report on and try to explain past and present developments, they are often solid and enlightening contributions to the understanding of human affairs. If and when they are biased, it is usually easy enough to detect the bias and make the necessary allowances. But when it comes to estimates of the consequences of technology and technological change for the future, the biases involved are often such pervasive components of what is being predicted that the future looks like Doomsday or the Golden Age, depending on the direction of the bias.

In general, writings about the future, whether by optimists or pessimists, have one axiom in common. Explicitly or implicitly, they argue that *unless we do something about this or that in one way or another,* the future will be what it is predicted to be or it will not be what it is predicted to be. Unless humane values are cherished, unless long-range planning is introduced, unless there is reform of governmental institutions, unless there is birth control, unless there is law and order, unless there is this or that, the predicted consequences, good or evil, are surely to occur.

Two examples must suffice, one from the establishment literature and one from the literature of the counter-culture. Simon Ramo—a Ph.D., one is informed by the title page of his *Cure for Chaos*—believes in the systems approach. "So severe are some of our problems today that chaos threatens," he says, and continues:

> The systems approach to the analysis and design of anything . . . will provide no facility of infinite capacity. But allowing for all of these factors that we know are there, granted man's shortcomings and a ceiling on his resources and on his understanding of himself, it will lead us to designs and operations that will at least not be chaotic. The systems approach, if it is used wisely, is, at the least, a cure for chaos.[5]

Theodore Roszak, also a Ph.D., is the author of *The Making of a Counter-Culture,* perhaps the most persuasive statement of what the counter-culture is about. "If the resistance of the counter-culture fails," Roszak prophesies,

> I think there will be nothing in store for us but what anti-utopians like Huxley and Orwell have forecast—though I have no doubt that these dismal despotisms will be far more stable and effective than their prophets have foreseen. For they will be equipped with techniques of inner manipulation as unobtrusively fine as gossamer. Above all, the capacity of our emerging technocratic paradise to denature the imagination by appropriating to itself the whole meaning of Reason, Reality, Progress, and Knowledge will render it impossible for men to give any name to their bothersomely unfulfilled potentialities but that of madness.[6]

Statements like these can be easily multiplied but there is no way of determining the validity of their explicit or implicit premises; the more distant the future, the greater are the benefits or disasters that are anticipated. While these statements have all the appearance of being valid, they are nothing more than justifications for action in the present that are given philosophical, theoretical, and even scientific respectability by being presented as inexorable consequences of contemporary trends. But trends have a way of reversing themselves and are not necessarily good indicators of the shape of things to come.

The trouble with futurology, however animated by radical, reformist, conservative, or reactionary predispositions, or anything else, is that because its predictions are predicated on contingencies presumably intervening between present and future, it is at best an exercise in self-fulfilling or self-denying prophesies. The "unless syndrome" is a guarantee that the futurologist will never be wrong. If things turn out as predicted, the contingent condition will undoubtedly be found to have occurred; if things do not turn out as predicted, the contingent condition will be found not to have occurred. But if this is so, then one should turn to the serious study of these contingent conditions—the "unless" of predictions—and let the future take care of itself. Continuously revising one's estimates of the future has the quality of astrology.

It certainly serves no good purpose to substitute one image of the future for another. Introducing new assumptions does not improve the quality of anticipation. The "unless syndrome" is at best a self-serving demand that something be done, and it serves perhaps as a stick for browbeating recalcitrants and opponents into doing it. This is the true meaning of what the latter-day Luddites of the counter-culture and the latter-day technocrats of the establishment are doing when they formulate their prognostications.

Yet, the future is important and images of the future are important precisely because they shape what is done in the present. Regardless of whether they are conscious or unconscious, assumptions about the future, like other biases, are built into research. Making one's images of the future explicit improves the quality and relevance of writing and research. But in constructing these images one should bring to the task the same spirit of disinterested inquiry that is cherished in research. The future should be inviolable. To use the future in the name of science in order to bring about change in the present is to abuse science. Under these conditions little or no credibility can be assigned to predictions.

It is for these reasons that Harold D. Lasswell's exceptionally self-conscious and disinterested formulation of the problematics involved in the study of the future is so appropriate. Long before the futurist craze of the last decade or so, Lasswell concerned himself with the future and its implications for both political science and public policy. He suggested that any problem-solving approach has five intellectual tasks which he characterizes as goal thinking, trend analysis, specification of conditions, projection, and the formulation of alternatives. All five tasks enter the formulation of a "developmental construct" which in its methodological sophistication sharply contrasts with the naïve images of the future to which we are treated in the literature on the impact of technology.[7] A developmental construct, Lasswell writes,

> is a speculative model in which the present is characterized as a transition between a selected pattern of events located in the past and a pattern imputed to the future. No claim of scientific validity is made for the model, although the present state of knowledge is taken into account in setting up the hypothesis. The developmental construct is not a simple extrapolation of recent trends, but a critical weighing of future outcomes considered as an interacting whole. By highlighting some major possibilities we may be led to revise our previous estimates of the situation and to guide our research and policy activities with a view to taking advantage of emerging opportunities for analysis, insight, and perhaps control.[8]

It is the image of the future, then, that guides what is done in the present by way of research or policy, and not the other way around as in the case of "unless propositions.'' A concern with the future impact of the com-com technology on politics derives from the need to guide research in the present. The com-com technology's effect on politics is of interest not because there is an immanent virtue in futurology, but because it can serve to give significance and direction to research in the present which, as Lasswell puts it, ''is characterized as a transition between a selected pattern of events located in the past and a pattern imputed to the future.'' The pattern imputed to the future is a proper subject of social-scientific investigation. For ''imputation'' is something less than prediction, yet something more than divination.[9]

Now, the strange thing that can happen on the way to the future is that it will prove shocking only in retrospect. The trouble with Alvin Toffler's book, *Future Shock,* does not lie in his data but in his divination. Toffler defines future shock as the ''dizzying disorientation brought on by the premature arrival of the future,'' and says that it ''may well be the most important disease of tomorrow.'' Like all good futurists, he protects himself by the usual contingent *unless:* ''Unless intelligent steps are taken to combat it, millions of human beings will find themselves increasingly disoriented, progressively incompetent to deal rationally with their environments.''[10] Needless to say, if the predicted future does not materialize, then obviously something has been done about it. In contrast to Toffler's expectations, precisely because modern man is living in a time of greatly accelerated rates of change, the future is always so close at hand that it is anything but shocking. Modern man is amazingly adaptable and readily accepts technological innovations. The contemporary young are nurtured on television; moon travel seems reasonable to them; and the com-com technology is something they will take in stride.

The exhilarating aspect of present-day technology is that one need not just contemplate the future but can, in effect, live it as it unfolds. The late fifties of this century were still the age of the desk calculator and the counter-sorter or, at best, the IBM 101. Indeed, computers seemed to be rather unwieldy things. In the early years of the computer there was endless talk about programming and compiling and debugging. One rarely hears this talk today.

Some years ago a conference with the intriguing title ''Information Utilities and Social Choice'' was held at the University of Chicago.[11] By this time, computers could store an almost endless amount of information; they could calculate ten to the seventh or eighth power as fast as man could; simultaneous access through time sharing and consoles had made it possible to be at two places at the same time; and ingenious programs and sub-routines were available for getting quick answers to one's problems. There was no talk about frustrations in using the computer in research as had been common in the early sixties. Instead, the talk was about something altogether new, something that had become technologically feasible but was still impractical—the interactive information utility. And the talk was not about what this utility could do in research, for its research uses were taken for granted; it was about the possible effects of the utility on politics in the real world. The future seemed to be right there in the conference room.

Present at the conference were two types of people. In one room were computer scientists and engineers; in another were social and political scientists. It was not clear what, in the joint concluding session, the two groups learned from each other; but the social scientists seemed to take more seriously what the computer people had to say about the future of the com-com technology than the computer people seemed to take seriously what the social scientists had to say about the consequences of the new technology for politics. The reason for this is very simple: it is much easier to comprehend technology than to comprehend political behavior. In general, the social and political scientists did not expect dramatic changes in political behavior and processes as a result of the interactive information utility, though they were sensitive to possible changes at the margins. And these marginal changes may yet be significant enough to make it mandatory to give them serious attention before they occur.

The description given here of the interactive information utility will be brief and stylized, to convey only some impression of what is being envisaged on the technological side. The interactive information utility is simply a two-way combination of computation and communication made possible by coaxial television or, as it is better known, Cable TV (CATV). Computation in this connection means the processing, storage, and retrieval of information; communication means the transmission of information through interaction between man and machine. The potentialities of the computer are now well known. Coaxial television will make possible the reception of communications on as many as forty to fifty channels. The two-way system involves, in addition to the TV set, some kind of typewriter or teletype board that permits instant communication between sender and receiver, be it man or machine. Existing prototype systems are reported to be able to handle as many as 10,000 messages in about one second.[12] In other words, the interactive information utility is only a technological extension of current man-to-man feedback systems between TV senders and receivers via telephone communication or the man-machine exchanges with which we are familiar.

The concern here is not with the technological aspects of the new utility or its economic feasibility. In regard to the former, one can assume that a decade or two from now CATV or narrow-casting will have effectively replaced broadcasting TV. The economic feasibility of the multi-channel system is still an open question; but let us assume that it has also been solved. From the point of view of those who see in the com-com technology the promises of increased societal democratization this is, of course, a crucial question. If the economics of CATV are such that only the well-to-do can avail themselves of the utility, its democratic communication potential is jeopardized. There are other problems as well. The concept of utility means not only that it must be purchased but also that it is subject to government regulation. But the information utility does not just distribute raw materials like electricity or water; it requires software support, that is, a programming language that is simple and largely self-defining so that it can be widely used; and it requires manageable and efficient organization of data. But, again, let us assume that all of these problems are solved and that the utility is a genuine facility for the entire population—the rich and the poor, the educated and the uneducated.[13] What are its likely consequences for political behavior and political processes?

One could, at this point, cite any number of rather naïve prognostications of the benign consequences of the com-com technology for democratic politics. A cynic might be inclined to write off these prognostications as a kind of sales pitch of the technologists. But this would be doing them an injustice. Many of them are sincere in their faith that the new utility would usher in a new Jeffersonian politics. As Don K. Price pointed out some time ago,

> Their ideal would be an egalitarian democracy, with all issues decided by votes of private citizens who have not been corrupted by service in the bureaucracy, and all of whom are earnestly studying science. The ideal has been depicted—with an admission of its lack of realism but still as an ideal—as a system of electronic communication in which every citizen could watch and listen to a Congressional debate and then register his vote instantaneously in a national referendum.[14]

Interestingly, Professor Price cites in this connection no other than Simon Ramo, Ph.D., who has already been mentioned as an advocate of the systems approach.[15] But one need not set up the technologist as a straw man. Professor Zbigniew Brzezinski, a responsible political scientist, has written a very interesting book, *Between Two Ages: America's Role in the Technetronic Era.* Brzezinski, speaking of the Constitution, is careful to point out that "needed change is more likely to develop incrementally and less overtly. Nonetheless, its eventual scope may be far-reaching, especially as the political process gradually assimilates scientific-technological change. Thus, in the political sphere the increased flow of information and the development of more efficient techniques of coordination may make possible greater devolution of authority and responsibility to the lower levels of government and society."[16] It is difficult to quarrel with this estimate, but in a footnote Brzezinski goes gung-ho into the future:

> These techniques could also be used to improve electoral procedures and provide for closer consultation between the public and its representatives. Existing electoral machinery in the United States—in regard to both registration and voting procedure—has simply not kept up with innovation in electronic communications and computation. Reforms (such as electronic home-voting consoles) to make it possible for representatives of the public to consult their constituents rapidly, and for these constituents to express their views easily, are both technically possible and likely to develop in view of growing dissatisfaction with present machinery. More

intense consultation, not necessarily only on the national level or only in regard
to political institutions, would further enhance the responsiveness of the American
social and political system.[17]

What is implied or anticipated here is a participative nightmare rather than the
good society.[18] Such enthusiasm for electoral and representational reform by
way of the com-com technology is at best simple-minded and at worst ill-
informed. Electoral and representational behavior in all their manifestations are
sufficiently complex not to be easily harnessed by even very sophisticated
technological gadgetry.

Any reasonable non-futuristic, yet future-oriented, discussion of the com-com
technology's impact on politics must proceed from three assumptions: first, that
technological change is more rapid than political and social change, and that
political organization is more resistant to change than technological organization;
second, that automata, their name notwithstanding, are not autonomous, and that
one better thinks of the com-com technology as an extension of man not different
from, except in scale, the fountain pen; and third, that if the com-com technology
is an extension of man and more easily changed than his behavior and social
organization, it is more likely that politics will have an impact on the technology
than the technology on the shape of politics. It follows that talk about the impact
of this or that technology really tries to say something about how man utilizes the
technology and what the consequences of his behavior are rather than what the
consequences of the technology are. This can be stated more explicitly: what one
is trying to anticipate when one talks about the impact of an item of technology
is really behavior in coping with the technological item. In other words, future
political behavior under the conditions of the com-com technology will be
adaptive or responsive behavior seeking to cope with these conditions. Personali-
zation of the computer is rampant in the popular media and, one may assume, in
the popular imagination. But this is not helpful in observing development.

The com-com technology is also not something like an earthquake or hurricane
that suddenly and unexpectedly creates a situation for which those affected are
altogether unprepared. The com-com technology is not a natural but a cultural
event prepared over decades of physical and human engineering. From the
abacus down, computing machines were handled, programmed, or controlled by
men and they were not something to which men had to adapt themselves
suddenly as they might to a natural catastrophe. It is correct to say that the
com-com technology will represent a new social enviroment. But a social environment is invariably a transactional situation in which the behavior of one party
to the transaction both conditions and is conditioned by the behavior of the other
party. Transactional behavior is always subject to the law of anticipated reactions—which is to say that one party behaves in response to the behavior of
another who has not yet behaved and whose as-yet-to-come behavior is a response

in turn to something that has not yet occurred. In the transactional environment of the com-com technology man has a decided advantage over the computer—for he created the computer and anticipated its response. The computer is unlikely to overcome this handicap.

Moreover, the transactional environment created by the com-com technology is ambiguous because its component dimensions—coaxial communication, on the one hand, and computerization, on the other—are antinomous. Coaxial communication is conducive to fragmentation, privatization, and pluralism of the social system. Many highly specialized channels are available for the dissemination of a great variety of messages that compete for the utility user's attention. The environment is a buyer's market, and the buyer—say, of a dozen channels—has a greater choice in turning a program off than is the case with today's broadcasting system. Instead of broadening the base of participation in political or public affairs programs, narrow casting may actually reduce the number of people tuned in, as they can switch to alternative programs more to their liking. Blacks may prefer to tune in black programs, Protestants Protestant programs, football enthusiasts football programs, opera buffs opera programs, meditators meditation programs, and so on. Because CATV has this potential, the com-com technology will have the effect of reinforcing tendencies toward social fragmentation, pluralism, and privacy.

If CATV is a centrifugal force, computerization of information is a centripetal force. In the exchange that takes place between those who control the computer and those who make inputs into the system, the former are more likely to gain than the latter. Rather than necessarily making for access of wider segments of the population to the tension points of political decision-making, the information received from the public and stored in the computer benefits the politically active stratum or its substrata more than the politically passive population. This implies, of course, that the transactional environment of the com-com technology has no decisive impact on the distribution of attention and influence in society. If anything, it may widen the gap between the politically active stratum and the mass population. The problem created by the interactive information utility is very much the same that faces the social indicator movement. The problem there is to determine just what indicators are to be chosen by whom for inclusion in the data bank. To argue that the storage capability of the computer is inexhaustible is no compelling argument for the collection of data if one raises the political question of utilization. It is surely not simply a matter of the pushing of a button by the potential user of a data information system to find out what he wants to know. To be politically useful, the information obtained through the interactive utility must be sifted, evaluated, and condensed. This gives the center of the system a great deal of power, and that an information system controlled from the center may degenerate into a misinformation system is a possibility not difficult to imagine. The check on misuse of information at the center is, of course, the behavior of people at the periphery of the communication network: by enabling audiences to turn off, the com-com technology's internal contradictions serve to neutralize the power of the center.

It is unfortunate that the study of the mass media of communication is now almost exclusively pursued by communication specialists who have a self-serving interest in making information the critical variable in the study of politics. While these specialists are indeed well qualified to study communication, their sense of politics is not disciplined by a science of politics. For instance, what are we to make of a statement that "if such a computer information system containing status information on all pending legislation could be as accessible to a poor black in Watts as it is likely to be to an oil lobbyist in Washington, he may have more incentive to participate in the political process non-violently?"[19] The implicit assumption that political violence is due to lack of education and information is not tenable. It only shows faith in the salutary potential of the educational process. Revolutions are not made by the ignorant but by those who know too much.

The problem in bringing the com-com technology to bear on political behavior is less a problem of providing relevant information than a problem of eliminating irrelevant information for the very simple reason, articulated by Anthony Downs, that information is expensive.[20] The com-com technology will not make information any less expensive to the ordinary citizen. If this is so, just what the com-com technology will do in politics hinges on an assessment of the data needs in political behavior—or, put in other words, on a model of political man. If the model is that of the rational, well-informed citizen, questions of data generation, storage, and retrieval, the building of data banks, access languages, and so on, will loom large. The ideal is that of a data-rich and expanding universe of information on which the enlightened legislator, political leader, or citizen can draw selectively for whatever he thinks he needs in decision making. If, on the other hand, the model of political man is that of the bewildered, confused, and possibly alienated citizen, interest centers in how the citizen or legislator can be protected from the helter-skelter overabundance of informational stimuli that may have caused his bewilderment in the first place. Attention turns to the evaluation and condensation of information as well as to the problem of political control of the com-com technology. The assumption here is, then, that the legislator or citizen does not necessarily know what he needs by way of information.

Both models and their implications for the com-com technology present dilemmas for democratic theory because any action maximizing the objective of the first model would minimize the objective of the second model. What one is confronting is a genuinely political issue; the two alternatives *seem* to be mutually exclusive. But are they really mutually exclusive under conditions of practical politics? An answer depends on one's definition of politics. If one means by politics such practices as compromising, bargaining, coalition build-ing, negotiating, persuading, and so on, the political environment is one in which alternatives that appear to be mutually exclusive can be syncretized into a new alternative. Unfortunately, there is not the kind of research that could be helpful in bringing about the political solution which a third alternative would represent. Very little is known about political man as an information gatherer and infor-mation digester under different conditions of information abundance or scar-city. For instance, it is not really known whether political bewilderment or alienation is even partly due to a person's inability to handle the enormous flow of often ambiguous or contradictory messages that reach him in a rela-tively open society. And it is not known whether a person saturated with infor-mation really comes to his decisions on the basis of the information he has or in spite of this information.

There is good reason to assume that too much information may be as detri-mental to intelligent political behavior as too little. Too much information may provide so many options to choose from that rational choice becomes impossible, and no choice is made. There is no easy way out of this dilemma. If all information is grist for the computer mill, the latent policy stance is surely one of intellectual laissez-faire. It may be the easy way out but a costly way. While traditional political liberalism has persuasively argued in favor of unrestricted freedom and access to information, one cannot avoid at least some attention to the political dysfunctions of an information system that recognizes no outer bounds. The laternative has already been alluded to: a controlled information system surely smacks of censorship and is unacceptable in a free society.

One of the chief troubles with the rosy pictures of the future that enthusiasts of the interactive information utility or other com-com technologies envisage is that they facilitate, encourage, or reinforce rather simple-minded models of politics. This is true of those models of politics that are built on assumptions of organiza-tional systems and subsystems, and of those models that make assumptions about participatory democracy. Moreover, both models are predicted on the further assumption that the users of the com-com technology—executives, legislators, or citizens—can ask the right kind of questions. The assumption is more viable for organizational than political behavior. The city manager or corporate executive must be expected to ask the right kind of questions; it is hardly possible to build an organization on the opposite assumption. But the assumption is less viable in political environments. Whether the citizen can ask the right questions is problem-atic. The populist assumption is that the voice of the people is the voice of God; but it is an open matter whether the citizen understands his informational needs. This is not to say that he misunderstands them; it is only to assume that he needs tutoring in identifying the questions he wishes to have answered. This, of course, is the case for representative government. Representative government reduces the public's information costs,[21] and representative government gives focus to the questions that at least the reasonably informed citizen can ask. The representative's problem, in turn, is somewhat different. The individual representative may know what his information needs are, but as his decision making is a collective act he must also know and understand the informational needs and sources of his colleagues. He is not only interested in knowing what other politicians say but also why they say it.

Assessing the impact of a technolgical innovation *on* a particular environment involves assessing it *in* that environment. This is so because no environment, and certainly not the human environment, is the passive recipient of technological inputs. Any discussion of the com-com technology's consequences for politics must calibrate into its prognostications a scientifically valid view of the political environment in which the presumed technological impact will occur. The political environment is characterized by conflict, competition, persuasion, bargaining, compromise, coalition building, consultation, and so on. This is a very volatile environment. It will not passively adapt to the com-com technology of the future but help shape that technology. Research on political behavior will be enriched if it raises questions that are oriented toward the new com-com technology and its potentialities; but it must also anticipate the possible effects of politics on the technology. Up to now, most of the models of politics extended into the technological future have been unduly simplistic. One hunch is that neither the garrison state nor participatory democracy will inevitably result from the linkage of communication and computerization.

2 POTENTIAL EFFECTS OF THE INFORMATION UTILITY

The participative polity projected as a potential result of the continuing computer revolution is not something that can be easily written off as science fiction. It may well be real enough, but I take a somewhat less than sanguine view of its beneficial consequences for a more tolerant and humane society. In fact, to state my bias at the outset, what I would anticipate is a participative nightmare rather than the good society. If simple-minded predictions were to come true, we would have a situation bringing Western history full circle: the "closed society" of the Greeks would at long last be realized by the closed society of the computer age. The democracy of the Greeks, in theory or practice, is not a very attractive prospect; had it not been for representative government, Western political development might never have taken off as it did. In short, the prospect of the computerized democratic and equalitarian polity makes me shudder to my liberal bones.

Now, I don't believe that the continuing computer revolution will have the predicted consequences. To make full use of the interactive information system made possible by the computer technology, citizens would have to be so well informed for meaningful political interaction to take place that they would have to give up almost any other pursuit of happiness. The Greek citizen, in lore at least, was all political animal; the modern citizen, we know all too well, is not. To put this in the more formal language of contemporary political theory, the availability of a computerized, interactive information system may involve costs that the citizen is unwilling to pay. He may be unwilling to pay them, even though they promise him participation in the political decision-making process, because it would not be rational to do so. Anthony Downs has persuasively argued that information costs in a democracy may at times be so high as to make non-participation in the political process the more rational strategy.[1]

It would be foolish of me to argue against the informational benefits that the future information utility could have in a system of government which, in the end, must seek its legitimacy in popular support and in what it does for the people; but what a government does for its people, or the support that it is given by the people, are not the sole criteria of its beneficence. Its wisdom, its justice, or its rationality are values as relevant as its legitimacy or authority.

Rationality is, perhaps, the most critical property of a viable political system. Certainly, Western societies pride themselves on rationality as the most characteristic attribute of their political decision-making processes. The availability of relevant, reliable, and valid information is considered in most models of choice making a necessary condition of rationality. Even if uncertainty or a degree of uncertainty is built into such models, the reduction of uncertainty through information-utilizing strategies is assumed to be an indication of rational behavior, and the rational strategist is advised to maximize his information sources. But, as I have already suggested, information retrieval may involve costs that are counter-productive from the perspective of rational choice. And this dilemma, I shall argue, confronts not only the citizen but also the governmental decision makers.

When information costs are unduly high and citizens therefore refuse to inform themselves, Downs postulates, "the whole concept of representative government becomes rather empty if the electorate has no opinions to be represented."[2] But Downs fails to see, as I shall suggest, that representative government in fact reduces information costs. Although Downs provides for this in his model of representation, it is largely ignored in inferences made from the model. The Downsian world is populated by disembodied actors who out-guess and out-calculate each other but rarely, if ever, interact physically or engage in transactions with each other. Downs is quite aware of this in saying that "uncertainty is so basic to human life that it influences the structure of almost every social institution. The government in a democracy is no exception to this rule."[3] It is for this reason that, willy-nilly, he must introduce representation into his model, even though his view of representation, being constrained by the model, is very limited: "To cope with uncertainty, it (the government) is forced to employ intermediaries between itself and its constituents."[4] Representatives are these intermediaries. The functions they perform stem from the relationship between government acts and individual utility functions. Because the government plans its acts by looking at individual utility functions and discovering what voters want, it needs representatives *of* the people who can simplify the otherwise impossible task of exploring every individual's utility function. Also, individuals decide how to vote by comparing the acts of government and the proposals of opposition parties. Therefore government sends its own representatives *to* the people to convince them that its acts are worthy of their approval. Other parties, of course, employ representatives to convince the people that the incumbents should be replaced.[5]

There is refreshing quality in the partially sophisticated, partially naïve view of the representational process that Downs outlines. That "uncertainty thus helps convert democracy into representative government" is the sophisticated part; that the government "employs, as a part of its own institutional structure, a group of men whose function is to scatter into the corners of the nation and discover the will of the people'' is the naïve part of the Downsian model.[6] In effect, Downs asks us to accept the individualistic version of representation made famous by John Stuart Mill. This version places great emphasis on the representative process as a source of accurate information about the people; but, as only one instance of representation, it is ''metapolitical,''[7] and, from the standpoint of practical conditions in the modern mass society, it is altogether utopian.

In the real world of contemporary politics, with its mass electorates and mass constituencies, the representative is something less than a purveyor and transmitter of popular preferences, if he ever was. Not even the most ardent advocate of a theory of representation which places a high premium on the information-gathering function can deny the pervasiveness of what Kenneth Janda has called ''mandate uncertainty.''[8] The representative as a transmitter of preferences is, from the perspective of a modern information utility, technologically obsolete. To expect him to be something that he cannot be is both bad political advice and bad political science. Granted, the representative needs information desperately, especially information about how his socially heterogeneous constituents feel, what they prefer, and what they want; but his need *for* information does not make him a good collector or transmitter *of* information. For whatever his representative role, the modern representative cannot possibly measure up to Edmund Burke's solemn injunction that ''it ought to be the happiness and glory of a representative, to live in the strictest union, the closest correspondence, and the most unreserved communication with his constituents.''[9] It matters not, for this purpose, to review whatever else Burke said about representation, and he had much to say. The point to be made is that the individual representative is not, and cannot be, a public opinion polling organization, an information storage system, and a computing facility. Yet, much of the talk one hears about representation, not the least by elected officials themselves, sounds as if this were a real option.

The thought is so beguiling that it is heady, especially if one contemplates the vast potential of a computerized, interactive information system. If the representative were nothing but a collector and transmitter of information, as he is in the Downsian model and all the other equally individualistic, if less elegant, models of representation, there would seem to be no need for him at all in the new world of the computer. In fact, it would seem that the computerized, interactive information utility of the future has solved the ''problem'' of representation by doing away with it. The participative polity would make the citizen's living room the seat of government.

The image is so absurd that I shall not pursue it further. The participative polity would, at best, be a vicarious democracy. At worst it would be a form of manipulated, conformist mob rule. But to denounce the image hardly serves a constructive purpose, for it is not unreasonable to assume that a computerized, interactive information utility can, and probably will, serve the representative process in a democracy. But to make it useful, one must entertain some other assumptions about representation than the simplistic notions inherited from the eighteenth and nineteenth centuries.

Although the governmental process is necessarily carried out by human actors, largely through a multitude of transactions between representatives and represented, representation in modern mass society is an eminently systemic phenomenon. Because it is a systemic phenomenon, it cannot readily be reduced to the level of individual relationships, though it undoubtedly emerges from these relationships. In other words, representation is not something that somehow "exists" at the micro level between representative and represented, but something that *emerges* at the macro level under certain conditions that are conducive to its emergence. It is not something that can be easily engineered, as the constitution builders of the nineteenth century believed, but something that may or may not occur in the wake of interactions between representatives and represented.[10] Whether it occurs cannot be easily inferred from formal government arrangements but must be ascertained empirically from one political system to the next. Representation may or may not happen, and whether it happens or not—whether it emerges—is a matter of a great many conditions in the political system.

This is not the place to state all of the conditions that make for or against the emergence of representation as a systemic property of the democratic polity. However, that the availability of an adequate information utility is not the least important among these conditions can hardly be controverted. More controversial, of course, is the question of just what purposes the information utility should serve as well as the question of just what an adequate utility would be. To answer these questions, the role of the representative agency in the informational process must be properly understood, just as it is necessary to understand the place of information in the representational process.

To suggest that the representational process is never better than the information that goes into it is not really saying very much. Lack of information is something about which representatives invariably complain, but it is a public stance that is justifiably suspect, for equally frequent is the complaint that, because of time pressure, the representative is unable to absorb all the information that does come to his attention. This theme is also suspect. Politicians are notoriously capable of wanting to have things both ways, but one should not discount either complaint out of hand. In combination, they may well be symptomatic of some basic trouble in the relationship between representational and informational processes.

It may be, for instance, that it is not so much lack of information as its inaccuracy and possibly irrelevance that troubles the representative. But if this is so, it does not necessarily follow that the fault lies with the information system. There is a tendency in our culture to blame almost all malfunctioning of interpersonal relationships on lack of communication or partial communication.

Communication becomes the *deus-ex-machina* solution for all of the world's troubles, from divorce to war, from juvenile delinquency to revolution. I take a somewhat dim view of such one-factor explanation.

Let me take another line. It may be argued that, his protestations notwithstanding, the representative himself is the source of his informational troubles. It is said sometimes that the politician hears with a "third ear." Now, whatever meaning the metaphor may have, this third ear can and often is a very deceptive device of information gathering. More often than not, the third ear hears what it wants to hear; it selects, screens, distorts, and omits. It would seem, therefore, that if representatives rely on their third ear, they are bound to make mistakes and get into political trouble. The implication, in turn, is that if the representative only had accurate information, his problems would vanish. He would become the true spokesman of his clientele and a wise decision maker to boot.

Alas, quite apart from once again making representation and information almost identical, this implication constitutes a profound miscomprehension of the representational process. Rather, I would argue that if the representative did not hear with a third ear, he would be so inundated with information as to become politically inefficacious and ineffective. In the current technical vocabulary, he would be a victim of information overload. Because on all political issues there is much truth on both sides, the full truth would incapacitate the representative as decision maker.

However, the political process in all its complexity, including the representational process, is not a quest for truth but a quest for reconciling conflicting interests. The task of reconciliation, especially as it is rooted in the representational process, is not the individual representative's burden. It is the burden of the representational system as a whole, and it is for this reason that representation must be conceived of as a systemic phenomenon that may or may not emerge. In other words, while at the level of the individual representative, the very nature of the representational task makes for "noise" in the channels of communication, this may not be the case at the level of the representational system. Precisely because each individual representative hears with a third ear, it is the great virtue of the broadly based representative body that it may or may not respond collectively to a variety of societal needs. Put differently, representation emerges precisely because each individual representative can and will respond selectively to the demands that come to his focus of attention. From this perspective, limited information, one-sided information, and perhaps even no information at all are as crucial to the emergence of representation as is full and accurate information. That information is selectively screened by individual representatives in terms of their personal predispositions or the pressures brought on them by constituents, clienteles and other sources—not least important among these being other representatives—should not be regarded as being dysfunctional. It makes representation as a systemic phenomenon the critical factor in governance that it is.

The individual representative, then, cannot be thought of as being simply the passive recipient of information that he somehow uses to his best lights as he tries to represent interests, makes decisions, and contributes to the resolution of conflict. Rather, he is himself an important actor in the information system, and he is not so much a collector or transmitter as a maker of information. He brings to public attention and to the attention of his colleagues what he thinks is in the interest of his own goals or the goals of his particular constituents or even the polity as a whole. It may be useful to him to conceal information as much as to reveal it. To expect him to be well-informed and even accurately informed on all matters on which he must decide is to ask not only the impossible but, from the systemic perspective, probably the undesirable. If he often listens only with the third ear and keeps his other two ears shut, it is because he may have to cut himself off from information or at least make it usable for his purposes.

I would argue, therefore, that a highly accurate, reliable, and complete information system is not *ipso facto* conducive to rational decision making in a representative democracy. On the contrary, from the societal perspective, it may actually be so costly as not to be a rational instrument of governance at all. It would be unduly costly because it could not be meaningfully utilized. Such utilization is severely circumscribed by the representational process. The representative need not know everything that he perhaps should know. But if he knew it, the representational process would become costly. But the representational process in fact reduces information costs by its built-in screening device—the limited capability of the representative to absorb and process all of the information that could be potentially his but is not.

I do not want to be misunderstood. I am not saying that the representative should not have at his disposal as full information as possible when and if he wants or needs it. I am saying that the representational process generates constraints of its own that restrict what the representative wants to hear or needs to hear. These constraints inhibit or promote representation as a systemic property of a political system. Under some conditions, therefore, maximizing the returns from a perfect informational utility may be unduly costly because they actually interfere with the emergence of representation and rational decision making. The great variety and complexity of the issues that face modern representatives, the time pressures that inexorably call for action, or the need to respond to political demands regardless of their soundness, make utilization of information in the technical sense, even when available, not a sufficient condition of rational decision making. Under these circumstances, the representational process as I understand it is not only cheaper than a full-fledged informational utility but also more conducive to effective governance.

I can now return to the two questions I raised earlier: what is the purpose of an information utility, and what is an adequate utility? It would appear from what I have said so far that the utility must be capable of being relevant to the representational process. In other words, if one approaches the questions I raised from a more sophisticated point of view of representation than that evident in individualistic models, it appears that two perspectives are involved. One perspective is more or less objective and solves the task of building an information utility relevant to the problems of representation from the technological side. In this perspective the utility would be politically neutral. The analogue of this perspective is, in effect, the expert, disinterested, disengaged, depersonalized information system that is multifunctional, very much like the classical, politically neutral bureaucracy which could be called upon to provide specialized knowledge and expert advice. Kenneth Janda has detailed how such a system could serve different levels of organization—the Congress as a whole, each chamber of the Congress, Congressional committees and individual Congressmen.[11] The adequacy of the system would be judged by its ability to provide maximum information at all times to its users.

There is no need for me to appraise at length the adequacy of an information system that is an analogue of the classical bureaucratic model of government. A technologically adequate system is a necessary, but not a sufficient, facility for the emergence of representation as a property of politics. A viable information system relevant to representation must be approached and appraised from a second and essentially subjective perspective. If representation involved nothing more than mirroring constituent preferences and providing factual information, one might as well replace the representative process with a computerized decisional apparatus, very much along the models of rational choice that need only be properly programmed to be operative. However, I have never heard the suggestion that this is feasible or desirable. Whatever the potential of a perfect information utility in the representational process may be, as Harold D. Lasswell so aptly put it as long as fifteen years ago, "even in an automatizing world some top-level choices must be made. In that sense at least, discretion is here to stay."[12] One might add that in a democracy these discretionary, top-level choices are eminently choices conditioned by the process of representation.

What I am arguing is, in essence, that the informational needs of the individual representative must be appraised in the context of the representational as a systemic process and not in the perspective of either an abstract model of individual, rational decision making or a bureaucratic model of government. These informational needs, in turn, seem to be largely a function of four variables. First, there is the degree to which the representational body serves in fact as the effective decision maker in the political system; second, there is the representative's position in the representative body—the degree to which he occupies a crucial gate-keeping position in the representational hierarchy; third, there is the degree to which the representative is personally interested and involved in the issues he is called upon to decide; and last, but not least, there is the degree to which constituency interests actively enter the representative's political calculus.

I shall deal only with this last variable, for it is critical for the emergence of representation as a systemic phenomenon. No hard and fast suggestions can be made as to just what information the individual representative should have to participate intelligently—a criterion somewhat less demanding than being rational—in the policy process. Too much information, I suggested earlier, may be as nonfunctional or even dysfunctional as too little information. It is the political salience of a particular policy issue to a particular representative that is most likely to determine the degree to which he will seek information in order to make judgments that are relevant to his representational function. And salience in politics, in turn, is largely a matter of considerations of party and constituency interests.

Whatever considerations in fact influence the representative as policy maker, it is convenient for him to attribute his policy stands, if not to his own conscience, to his constituency interests. While it is probably false to assume that representatives will invariably try to please their constituents, an aroused constituency can have an important impact on the representative; but, in fact, constituencies are rarely aroused. Paradoxically, this may be due in part to the successful functioning of representation—and this successful functioning may be due to the representative's anticipation of constituency reactions to his policy choices. While the "law of anticipated reactions" makes it difficult to trace the flow of cause and effect in the representational process, it is not unreasonable to assume that information has had something to do with it. As Karl Deutsch, suggesting relevant research in this area, points out, we cannot find out, of course, except after the event, how well a politician or ruler has anticipated such reactions, but we can find out well in advance of the event what efforts were made to collect the relevant information, through what channels it was brought to the point of decision, and what chance the decision makers had to consider it at all.[13]

Many issues facing representatives have low salience for them because the conditions of high salience—articulated demands from a broad section of the population—are missing. Not even the best information system in the world can generate political demands. As a result, the individual representative is likely to give his attention to matters that loom more prominently in his mind as he sets his own priorities. While this outcome may facilitate his representational tasks as an individual, it deprives the representational body of significant inputs, but also frees it from some of the political constraints that might otherwise be present. This situation is different from the kind of bargaining situation among representatives that takes place in policy areas where the stakes are seen as politically significant for survival in the future, especially in constituencies that are highly competitive. The representative as an individual can more readily take the role of trustee, and the representative body can respond more readily to a self-defined image of constituency interest, than in matters in which the representational process is subject to the pulls and pushes of partisan mutual adjustment. But, in contrast to the latter, the information costs are probably much higher. As Charles E. Lindblom has argued, "partisan mutual adjustment imposes on no one the heroic demands for information, intellectual competence, time, energy, and money that are required for an overview of interrelationships among decisions."[14]

If this line of thought is correct, it follows that the effect of the information utility on the representational process will vary with the kind of representational process that ensues in the course of the utility's functioning. If the information system, through anticipating reactions, makes for a quiescent representational process, the costs may be extremely high—so high, in fact, that paying them would not be economical. In other words, an expensive and presumably efficient information system would have the effect, on one hand, of increasing the individual representative's political security but reducing the representational body's collective responsiveness; on the other hand, an ineffective informational system might increase the need of partisan mutual adjustment in the representational process and thereby reduce information costs. It cannot be simply assumed, therefore, that maximizing the informational utility will automatically facilitate representation, if by representation is meant collective responsiveness and responsibility to constituencies.

Information *per se* is not necessarily conducive to representation, if representation is valued because it tends to bring about collective rather than individual rationality under certain conditions of the real world which the methodological, individualistic theorists rarely take into account in building their rational models of politics or fail to include in their calculations altogether. A full and complete interactional information utility providing each individual representative with accurate data about his constituency interests would lead to a situation described, in another connection, by Mancur Olson as one in which "no one legislator can feasibly trade off one interest in favor of another, and therefore the degree of compromise necessary to a continuing democracy may be unattainable."[15] In short, the interactive information system will, in my judgment, have only limited bearing on the problematics of representation in a democracy.

3 TECHNOLOGY AND THE FEAR OF CIVILITY

Hyperbole is the trademark of writing on technology and its impact on human affairs.[1] My indiscretion in using a mysterious or sensational title may be a case of epidemic infection. My intent, of course, is not to be mysterious or sensational. Rather, it is irony that I have in mind. Although technology is usually the manifest target, it is a fear of the politics of civility rather than of technology that pervades much contemporary writing on the social impact of technology. To irony must be added paradox. The politics of civility is feared not only by those who dislike technology, but also by those who see in technology the tool for curing the social problems that stem from its impact.

My argument rests, of course, on my conception of what a politics of civility means. Let me begin, therefore, with a very brief and at best only suggestive explication—without being, I hope, either banal or pedantic; and lest I be misunderstood, let me emphasize that what I am explicating is an "ideal-type" normative construct, in Max Weber's sense, and not an empirical type descriptive of American reality. That reality still more approximates the ideal type than it does not, I think; but it would be foolish to deny tendencies in American politics that in fact threaten it. Nevertheless, the formulation of an ideal-type construct of "civil politics" is the particular contribution that political scientists can make to the debate between technologists and antitechnologists over the role of politics in modern technological society.

The politics of civility as I think of it, refers to a broad range of potential behavioral patterns that can be expressed by such participles as persuading, soliciting, consulting, advising, bargaining, compromising, coalition building, and so on—in other words, forms of behavior in which at least two actors stand in a mutually dependent relationship to each other. Each actor is dependent on the other actor because each presumably has at his disposal the means to counter the behavior of the other. If the means are not present, the relationship is not one of mutual dependence. For instance, the relationship between prisoner and guard is, by this definition, not political, unless the prisoner through ingratiating behavior can elicit a favor from the guard. In that case, ingratiating is a form of political behavior on the prisoner's part that also serves the guard's interest because he values the prisoner's compliance to his own orders. In a civil relationship, then, the interaction is reciprocal, though not necessarily symmetrical, in that both actors gain from it. By way of contrast, withholding information from a superior, a tactic said to be not uncommon in bureaucracies, is not political because only one actor gains from the relationship. If the superior learns of his subordinate's treachery and dismisses him, the interaction is not political.

Politics is not limited to uniquely political institutions because I do not think uniquely political institutions exist. It is more common in legislatures than in administrative agencies or more common in parties than in courts of law, but it can be found in all kinds of human organizations, including even those that finally are based on the principle of strict hierarchy—say the Catholic Church—or on the principle of strict unanimity—say the Quaker meeting. The politics of such organizations is simply invisible. In any case, politics as I understand it, is predicated on mutually advantageous conduct in which neither actor can influence the behavior of the other actor without reciprocating in one way or another. This means, of course, that the relationship is one of mutual consent. Consent based on an expectation that one's action will call out deprivation or punishment is not political. By implication, then, politics so understood is feared when it is thought of as not exclusively contributing to or even interfering with an actor's goals. If these goals are considered unobtainable except through force, fraud, deceit, manipulation, and other forms of unilateral behavior, the introduction of civil politics into a relationship is unwelcome, for this would mean that the relationship will be uncertain because reciprocal conduct may or may not be forthcoming.

I realize, of course, that this definition of politics is restrictive. By excluding such forms of behavior as coercing, confronting, deceiving, manipulating, and so forth, I seem to be excluding from the range of politics types of conduct that, more often than not, are characteristic features of societal existence and transformation. Indeed, some theorists make just these forms of behavior the quintessence of politics. They see politics as a form of conflict whose outcome is inevitably and ultimately determined by domination, confrontation, manipulation, or violence. I would not want to banish these universal forms of behavior from the range of phenomena to which the term politics is applied, but they constitute a class of political patterns that is distinctly different from those that I subsume under the class called the "politics of civility."

The politics of civility is difficult both to explain and, consequently, to live by. I harbor few illusions about why it is that in the history of mankind the politics of civility has been a relatively rare occurrence. I certainly entertain no optimistic assumptions about inevitable progress toward the worth and dignity of man. Reluctantly I must agree with those who see the politics of civility not as the outcome of mass democracy but as an attribute of a minority always exposed to those sanctions which a majority can enforce if sufficiently aroused by the ineptitude or unresponsiveness of the governing few. If the fears of conservative critics of democracy have not materialized, it is largely due to the fact that the masses have been rarely aroused. If anything, their apathy or quiescence in political matters, at least until now, has made possible the cultivation of the politics of civility.

I am using the word cultivation self-consciously. The politics of civility is not something that can be invented or adopted like a gadget produced by human technology—say a planning-programing-budgeting system. Such a system is an artifact of technology that, upon invention and application requires greasing, oiling, and repair. The politics of civility, by way of contrast, cannot be made or unmade at whim, nor can it be repaired like a machine. Rather, the politics of civility is something that grows and is cultivated. It is, moreover, something that cannot be neatly packaged in a simplifying ideology. It cannot be expressed or communicated by any ready formula. In fact, its very elusiveness contributes to that fear-arousing quality which bothers those whose simple-minded ways of doing things it obstructs and who, being averse to learning the ways of political civility, are frustrated wherever and whenever it has a chance to prevail.

The politics of civility involves, then, a number of cultivated characteristics. Let me spell out at least two of these characteristics without being exhaustive yet remaining minimally suggestive.

First, the politics of civility is based on sensitivity to the complex relationship between means and ends, between procedural and substantive rationality, between the causes and purposes of human action. It recognizes that these relationships are, perhaps, so interdeterminate and even indeterminate that they are to a large extent a matter of subjective belief. At best much social and political behavior is based, in the words of Justice Oliver Wendell Holmes, on wagering one's salvation on some unproved hypothesis. There is, therefore, little room for ideology in the politics of civility. This is not to say that it is unaffected by values. It is to say that these values are immune to the kind of forcible ordering that the notion of ideology implies.

Moreover, assuming interdetermination and indeterminacy of human conduct, the politics of civility is predicated on tolerance of ambiguity. Tolerance of ambiguity is a psychological art that does not come easily and that, we have learned, is deeply rooted in personality. But it is something that can be learned, and the politician who practices the politics of civility has learned it. Tolerance of ambiguity is its own reward, provided of course that it is not confused with tolerance of intolerance. This is something that those who fear the politics of civility fear a great deal. For they know that the politics of civility has its own ways of handling intolerance, uncertain as these ways may be.

Second, the politics of civility is a mature politics. Maturity is the opposite of immaturity. It seems to me, and I think child psychology bears me out, that a child is preoccupied almost exclusively with what he wants, with his own self. Although he will be well aware of factors in his environment which might prevent his satisfaction, he is not concerned with the repercussions of his seeking satisfaction on his surroundings. In this connection he is thoughtless in a pure sense of the term. He is the focal center of the only world he knows. His spontaneous reaction to anything that thwarts his desires is to take it personally—to blame, resent, attribute wrongness or unfairness, have temper tantrums, and so on. He is not, in short, a civil being. He has no conception of being an integral part of society whose proper operation depends significantly on his behavior or of having responsibilities to others. Society is felt, rather, to be outside his self and to be simply useful or obstructive in the satisfaction of the demands of his self.

Maturity chiefly consists—if I have sufficiently suggested what is an immature attitude—in the habitually exercised capacity to respond to others and events without the demands of the self constituting the sole criterion according to which to behave or to make judgments. Put another way, maturity involves the recognition of the situation outside the self in contrast to the demands of the self; and while both are very real and important, they are distinct and separable. Using the term maturity in this way, the politics of civility recognizes and accepts the real world. True, most of us, in some degree, remain children all our lives. But most of us have in varying degree achieved maturity in our family lives, in our relationships with our work associates and neighbors. We have achieved the politics of civility when we are capable of asking not only "What is in it for me?" but also "What can I do for you?" It is out of these two simple questions that the politics of civility is born. If we ask only one of the questions, there is no politics as I understand it. Asking only "What is in it for me?" means a strategy of egotism that is bound to fail as it runs into the egotism of another; asking only "What can I do for you?" means a strategy of charity that in the end cannot deliver what it promises.

These remarks about what I mean by the politics of civility must suffice. But, it seems to me, that two groups, though relating themselves to the social problems of high technology in different ways, share a common fear of the politics of civility. First are the social critics or advocates of what is being called the counter-culture.[2] And second are those technologists who make a virtue of what their critics allege about them by calling them technocrats. Both groups share a fear of civil politics, and I think for the same reasons. Their fear of the politics of civility, in turn, makes both groups ineffective actors in the real world of politics.

The technologists of the establishment and the antitechnologists of the counter-culture have in common that their differing utopias are variously antipolitical yet properly embellished by an ambiguous vocabulary about democracy. I shall use the notion of technology broadly, including what is called applied science. Applied science is a more congenial concept than technology in the weak ideological environment of America because it gives the enterprise an aura of authority, impartiality, and credibility. In fact, this environment has at times the effect of making politics distrust itself. As Don K. Price, an astute observer of the science politics scene for two decades, has pointed out, "The emphasis on research as a preliminary to governmental action comes, of course, from an unwillingness to permit the government not only to answer a question arbitrarily, but even to define the issue, present its views, and manage the administrative machinery. This unwillingness to take the answers from established authority leads to a tremendous use of research as a basis of decisions at all levels."[3]

What Price observed in the early fifties has not reduced the technologists' fear of politics. Indeed, as they have become increasingly involved in politics, their distrust may well have increased. For they have learned that political victories are invariably followed by political defeats, and that the game of politics is different from the game of technology. In general, most technologists are willing to leave politics to the politicians; but some tend to believe that it is possible, if not desirable, to substitute technological for political ways in the solution of the problems that have been created by technology; or at least they find if difficult to accept that what is technologically feasible may not be socially desirable or politically viable.

I cannot quarrel with what is called technology assessment which means, despite its neutrally sounding name, not only the prediction but also the evaluation of the social consequences of technology. But evaluation of the consequences of technology is a political matter, and technology assessment is no substitute for political judgment. Technology assessment, like other efforts at appraisal in such areas as law enforcement, drug abuse, child welfare, government organization, and so on, seems to have the effect of taking politics out of what are basically political problems. National commissions to deal with this or that societal difficulty have been plentiful; yet all their pretense of objective research barely disguises their political character. As one observer stated 25 years ago, "Presidential commissions have been weakened in prestige by efforts to engage in fact-finding in matters that are socially and economically controversial. In these cases . . . it must be recognized that they can't find facts, they can only compromise."[4] But I doubt that the matter is so seen either by the experts called upon to bail the government out or by those who seriously expect visible pay-offs from the application of scientific expertise and intelligence.

A good example is a recent article on "Taming Technology" by Lewis M. Branscomb, director of the National Bureau of Standards. Branscomb is sensitive to the anonymity accompanying technological specialization, the dispersion of responsibility associated with mass production, and the interdependence of social subsystems like power, communication, health services, transportation, food production, or peace-keeping. A breakdown in any of these subsystems creates conflicts that endanger the society as a whole. The courts, Branscomb feels, cannot do the job of conflict resolution, and class-action suits will not do either. "There remains the arena of politics," he writes. "But our democratic political system can carry only a limited burden of conflict resolution."[5] Rather, conflict resolution "must come from a combination of research, of responsible private action, and astute public policy—all carried on within a rational framework. . . Research, once primarily a task to generate new technology, will in the 1970's increasingly be needed to support the formulation of policy and techniques for dealing with technology intelligently."[6]

What Branscomb offers is not only a faith in technology but an accompanying distrust of politics. The suggested procedure, he recognizes, "may produce a solution that is politically hard to sustain. But it is the rational procedure." The government, however, "accepts the solution that most easily survives politically."[7] This acceptance, clearly, is not to his liking; yet, the reason he gives is not that politics interferes with what he calls technology's "rational procedure," but that it threatens democracy:

> The difficulty with this rather traditional pragmatic approach is that once government has assumed the responsibility for determining the technological restraints under which all manufacturers must operate, government must also be responsible for the performance of the resulting product. And if it turns out that the public purpose—be it safety or environmental protection—that was the basis for regulation is not in fact served, public confidence in the possibility of taming technology through democratic processes is dealt another blow.[8]

Branscomb's prediction, like all such predictions, is a self-denying prophecy. "Accurate, credible, objective measurements will prove essential to the regulation of technology in the future . . . Unless dramatic progress is made, we may find that, even though technological fixes exist, we cannot administer a policy of public regulation under democratic principles and legal procedures."[9]

It may well be that without technological fixes democracy is doomed. But it may also be that without political fixes technology will get nowhere. This, it seems to me, is the lesson to be learned from the fate of planning-programing-budgeting systems (PPBS), in the Department of Defense and elsewhere. Here is a technology of decision making which, in ignoring politics, ignores what is probably the critical variable in the policy process. PPBS represents a logical structure that can neither be accommodated to the logical structure of politics nor absorb that structure. James Schlesinger, an economist and at the time assistant director, Bureau of the Budget, has seen the issue clearly:

> With perhaps a tinge of self-satisfaction on the part of its practitioners, systems analysis has been advertised as the application of logical thinking to broad policy issues. The implication is that logic comes in only one disguise. Yet, whatever the doubts of those who seek to rationalize politics, the political process is dominated by a species of logic of its own, one that diverges from the brand germane to systems analysis. The domain of politics is a far broader system than that to which systems analysis is typically applied.[10]

The perspective of PPBS is long-run, but the perspective of politics is short-run. In politics, Schlesinger continues, "one is engaged in mobilizing support by words and actions over a wide range of ill-defined issues. The ultimate criterion will remain the psychological and voting responses of the general electorate and of important pressure groups. Positive responses in this realm are only irregularly correlated with those actions preferred on the basis of cost-benefit criteria."[11] In retrospect it is almost incredible to believe that the Department of Defense planners not only ignored politics, but that they succeeded in selling their technology to a politically savvy president. To appreciate how technologists get that way, one must consult an authority who is neither ambivalent toward politics nor innocent of politics.

Professor B. F. Skinner is, of course, a controversial authority. In his utopian novel, *Walden Two,* Skinner presents a utopia where human behavior is scientifically controlled for presumably benign purposes.[12] And in his prose writing he has vigorously defended the claim that a science of human behavior is not only possible, but that it should be employed to control human behavior. Skinner's argument is revealing because he seems to be using a political argument against politics without really doing so.

Why, Skinner asks, are opponents of scientific control of human behavior so alarmed? They are alarmed, he says, because "the control of human behavior has always been unpopular." This aversion to being controlled, he continues, "has been exploited to good purpose in what we call the philosophy and literature of democracy. The doctrine of the rights of man has been effective in arousing individuals to concerted action against governmental and religious tyranny."

It is difficult to say whether Skinner approves, but to judge from what follows he does not, for he makes clear that the vocabulary of democracy "spells trouble for any science which may give birth to a powerful technology of behavior. Intelligent men and women, dominated by the humanistic philosophy of the past two centuries, cannot view with equanimity what Andrew Hacker has called 'the specter of predictable man'."[13] These attitudes, he concludes, "have already interfered with the free exercise of a scientific analysis, and their influence threatens to assume more serious proportions."[14]

It is easy to see why the scientific and technological community despairs of Professor Skinner's candor, for he speaks the unspeakable. Moreover, Skinner's sophistry is sophisticated. His technique is to present a very narrow definition of political control: "The state is frequently defined in terms of the power to punish, and jurisprudence leans heavily upon the associated notion of personal responsibility."[15] But take away punishment and the notion of personal responsibility, as a psychological technology of behavior control would, and there is no need to be afraid of control. "When governments resort to other techniques (for example, positive reinforcement), the concept of responsibility is no longer relevant and the theory of government is no longer applicable."[16]

His critics, Skinner complains, ignore the fact that the utopia described in *Walden Two* is benign. They simply oppose planning. "And this, to the child of the democratic tradition, spoils it all." He admits that "the dangers inherent in the control of human behavior are very real."[17] But, he argues, "brute force and deception, for example, are now fairly generally suppressed by ethical practices and by explicit governmental and religious agencies. A similar countercontrol of scientific knowledge in the interests of the group is a feasible and promising possibility."[18]

This development is, of course, a pious hope at best, and antitechnologists are right in distrusting it. Skinner attacks politics, it seems to me, because it is likely to be a disturbing factor in his utopia in which men march to the siren calls of positive reinforcement engineered by the technologists of human behavior. What makes his position so insidious is that in attacking politics Skinner invokes the authority of science. One must listen carefully to appreciate this fact: "The slow growth of the methods of science, now for the first time being applied to human affairs, *may* mean a new and exciting phase of human life to which historical analogies will not apply and in which earlier political slogans will not be appropriate."

By rejecting the relevance of historical experience and reducing politics to presumably obsolete slogans—like, one may infer, the rights of man—Skinner satisfies himself that democrats resist the new techniques of control only because they cling to "outmoded means to an end."[19] For the essence of politics is control: "All men control and are controlled. The question of government in the broadest possible sense is not how freedom is to be preserved but what kinds of control are to be used and to what ends."[20] This statement, certainly, is as blunt an expression of the technological approach to politics as any. If the ends are benign, they presumably justify control by manipulation; and if in the process the obsolete notion of political responsibility is sacrificed, so be it and all to the better, because positive reinforcement will do the job of control in a scientific manner.

I have paid so much attention to Skinner not because his antipolitical candor is prototypical but because it is not. If some engineers, technologists, systems analysts, or operations researchers were equally candid, I suspect that they would come out as Skinner does. However the pure technocrat looks at things, it is perfectly understandable why he must take a dim view of the politics of civility. The imprecise, volatile, and kaleidoscopic quality of this politics makes the task of the technologist and synoptic planner admittedly difficult.[21] But a more subtle explanation of why politics is repugnant to the technologist is available. Let me go to Francis Bacon's utopia, *New Atlantis,* to suggest the root of the technologist's attitude.[22]

The *New Atlantis* was ruled by an academy of scientists, called Solomon's House, that consisted of thirty-six members and exercised power collegially. As one commentator has pointed out, "Bacon was so sure of agreement on the part of the fellows as to scientific truth and its proper utility that he did not propose an odd number of members of the house or try to make a majority always possible."[23] The technological fix that Bacon envisaged was, moreover, immune to both natural catastrophe and political decay because its goal was to promote inventions, based on the methods of science, that guaranteed its citizens freedom from the vicissitudes of nature and society. Solomon's House could decide which inventions should be made accessible to the state and which ones not. Its unlimited wisdom in this respect would protect society from what today we call technology's undesirable side effects or spin-offs.

The *New Atlantis* was a depoliticized utopia in which all problems could be solved by the consensual process of science. I do not think it is farfetched to say that some of our modern technologists and scientists, trained as they are to accept the consensual character of science, believe that science through the application of technology can solve not only scientific but also social and political problems. Indeed, is it not reasonable to assume that scientific problem solving is superior to political problem solving? A scientific law is established when most scientists agree to it; conflict among scientists immobilizes science, but a solution that is not consensual, as a scientific law must be consensual, is not a solution. Unlike politics, science cannot live with its unsolved problems. Understandably, scientists and technologists are impatient with the drawn-out and continuing processes of bargaining, compromise, and majority-building that characterize the politics of civility. That the needs of science and technology, on the one hand, and the needs of government and society, on the other hand, are complementary is an assumption, that, I think, is shared by most scientists and technologists, regardless of whether they approve or disapprove of the application of a particular technology.

Of course certain other scientists and technologists do not underestimate the importance of politics—indeed, they play the political game as well as any other interest-group lobbyist. The dropping of the atomic bomb in World War II had a profound impact on the science community. Wherever they stood in the matter of the decision to drop the bomb, scientists could no longer assert that their scientific work and its technological applications were beyond politics.[24] The scientific community's concern with politics was real; neither science nor technology was any longer as immune from social and political criticism as it had been earlier. As criticism of scientific involvement in the Vietnam War and an awareness of the ecological problem spread in the mid-sixties, scientists and technologists became increasingly sensitive to politics. Yet, in their new-found discovery of the political process, some of them tend to substitute a kind of democratic perfectionism for technological utopianism. Indeed, the discovery of democracy makes them inadvertent bed-fellows of some antitechnologists whose remedy for the evil consequences of technology is "participatory democracy." I have heard some scientists seriously argue that the American people should have been consulted before the bomb was dropped on Japan, apparently on the assumption that the people would have opposed the decision. Popular consultation about the bomb might have made some scientists and engineers feel less guilty in the aftermath, but I doubt that the decision would have been different. Let us assume that the making of the bomb had been publicly announced, that a national debate had been held, that citizens had been able to form an opinion, and that a plebiscite had taken place. I venture to "post-dict" that in the context of the war both the production of the bomb and its utilization would have received enthusiastic popular support. In fact, I would argue that a contrary decision would have had more of a chance under organizational arrangements other than those of participatory democracy. There are certainly many alternatives of political participation and control between autocratic and secret decision making concerning the application of technology, on the one hand, and participatory democracy, on the other. The confrontation of technocracy and democracy, it seems to me, makes for a politically nonviable dualism.

In the literature critical of technology and its social consequences, it is not always clear whether technocracy is technology or whether it is the outcome of technology. It is also not clear just what kind of political order one should expect when the machines have been smashed and the threat of technocracy has been averted. In the end, one gets the feeling that what is involved is the kind of "revolution for the hell of it" that Abbie Hoffman has in mind.[25] But not many critics take up this battle cry, and most settle for a rather gloomy view of the shape of things to come. An exception is Theodore Roszak, whose antitechnological counter-culture is, in fact, an antipolitics.

The Making of a Counter-Culture is dedicated to the young—not all the young, Roszak concedes, and perhaps only a minority of university students. "Yet," he writes, "no analysis seems to make sense of the major political upheavals of the decade other than that which pits a militant minority of dissenting youth against the sluggish consensus-and-coalition politics of their middle-class elders."[26] I shall be doing Roszak an injustice by selective quoting, for he has many interesting things to say about technocracy, liberation, Zen Buddhism—which he likes—psychodelic experience—which he does not like— shamanism, and other aspects of the counter-culture; but my article is not a book review, and I am merely trying to convey an antitechnologist's antipolitical stance.

"Old-style politicking," Roszak concedes, may be necessary to cope with the Vietnam War or racial injustice, but

> the paramount struggle of our day is against a far more formidable, because far less obvious opponent, to which I will give the name "the technocracy" . . . In the struggle against *this* enemy, the conventional tactics of political resistance

have only a marginal place, largely limited to meeting life-and-death crises. Beyond such frontline issues, however, there lies the greater task of altering the total cultural context within which our daily politics takes place.[27]

I find Roszak's references to "old-style politicking" and "conventional tactics of political resistance" somewhat puzzling, but they are simply diversionary. For, in effect, he criticizes technocracy—among other things—because it fails to get rid of politics. Speaking of the "other Americans" not yet cut in on the country's material advantages, he expresses his concern: "But, at last (why should we doubt it?), all the disadvantaged minorities are accommodated. And so the base of the technocracy is broadened as it assimilates its wearied challengers. It might almost be a trick, the way such politics works."[28] The passage is paradoxical; it is difficult to say whether it is abhorring the admirable or admiring the abhorrent.

It is also difficult to say where Roszak comes out. He invidiously compares a presidential convention with the rites that hippies improvise. On the one hand, "A presidential convention or campaign filled with phonied-up hoopla is an obvious example of a debased ritual meant to cloak disreputable politicking with a democratic sanction."[29] On the other hand, "The tribalized young gather in gay costume on a high hill in the public park to salute the midsummer sun in its rising and setting. They dance, they sing, they make love as each feels moved, without order or plan. . . . All have equal access to the event; no one is misled or manipulated. Neither kingdom, nor power, nor glory is desperately at stake."[30] It would be a mistake, Roszak continues, to dismiss "such merry displays as so much marginal *joi de vivre*, having no political relevance." Something about it is sacred, "and to this something sacred which stands above all men, causes, regimes, and factions, all are allowed equal access. Could this not be the ultimate expression and safeguard of a participative democracy, without which the popular control of institutions might always be corrupted by partisan interest or deference to expertise?"[31] The simultaneous reference to "partisan interest" and "deference to expertise" and their corruptive power is revealing. There is the danger of temptation because

> the technocratic order can adapt itself to the purpose of entrenching itself ever more deeply in the uncoerced allegiance of men. This is the sort of insight our angriest dissenters tend to miss. . . . They quickly draw the conclusion that the status quo is supported by nothing more than bayonets, overlooking the fact that these bayonets enjoy the support of a vast consensus which has been won for the status quo by means far more subtle and enduring than armed force.[32]

Unfortunately, Roszak does not tell us what the "means far more subtle and enduring than armed force" are, but I suspect they are the "sluggish consensus-and-coalition politics" to which he referred earlier. Roszak's explicit target is technocracy; his implicit target is a politics, which, he suggests, makes technocracy possible. It is the politics of civility more than technology that stands between the harsh realities of the present and the dreams of the counter culture. The counter-culture is antipolitical. Roszak has sympathy for, but does not expect much from, the protest movement; I would add that it can give its participants only a false sense of political efficacy. It is the tragedy of recent years that the vitality of democratic reassertion and the legitimate demand for redress of grievances were exhausted, in the name of participatory democracy, in sit-ins, lie-ins, mill-ins, tent cities, freedom parties, communal wakes, protest marches, strikes that are not strikes, non-negotiable demands, and finally indiscriminate bombings. Two things may be said about these tactics. First, they became increasingly arbitrary and goal-free fads, examples of a typically American cultural tropism. Because the bus system of Montgomery, Alabama, could be effectively boycotted, or because lunch counters could be opened up by sit-ins carried on by a particular group of people at a particular historical moment, it does not follow that draft boards or police stations can be brought to their knees by similar tactics. Like the child who wants what he wants when he wants it, the politics of confrontation increasingly ignores the relationship between means and ends—in part because the means do not really fit sometimes vague, sometimes unrealistic ends, in part because the ends, however vague or unrealistic, seem so totally perfect and correct that any means, even if inappropriate, will do. The choice of tactics becomes a blind and random trial-and-error process; if one thing does not work, try another.

Second, like the child, antipolitics has no sense of real time. If, as the protest movement's more responsible spokesmen argue, the troubles besetting American life are deep-rooted, it is most unlikely that they can be eradicated in the short run by sporadic demonstrations, confrontations, thrashings, and bombings. Not only are these tactics self-defeating, but they are unlikely to hold together crowds of people whose motivations for participation are highly diverse and in many cases nonpolitical. Protest politics employed at the right time, at the right place, and with the right means may be politically effective, but only if it is seen as a complement of and not as a supplement for the politics of civility. If it is elevated into and sanctified as a principle of something called participatory democracy, vaguely defined and indiscriminately used, it expresses little more than a fear of civil politics.

Now, let me emphasize that this fear is by no means an unrealistic aspect of the participative politics. It may be its most realistic, if irrational, component. Two examples must suffice. First, we are told, sometimes even by United States senators, that the "system" has failed and "must be turned around." Indeed, I agree that the system has failed to respond to the self-appointed minority of saviors who claim to speak for "the people." The majority of the American people, as far as I can tell, is apparently not ready or willing to do away with injustice, poverty, urban blight, militarism, or imperialism either by taxing itself or by refusing to pay taxes, whichever is called for. If we are in trouble, as I think we are, it is not because the system has failed but because it seems to be muddling through more or less successfully. If one wishes the system to fail, one has indeed good reason to fear the politics of civility.

Second, there is the fear that, sooner or later, civil politics will co-opt and, presumably, corrupt those who are willing to play by the rules of the game. The system is full of temptations. There is a good deal of realism in this fear also. As originally used by Philip Selznick, co-optation is "the process of absorbing new elements into the leadership or policy-determining structure of an organization as a means of averting threats to its stability or existence."[33] But it also means, as Bennet W. Berger has pointed out, "the mechanism through which minorities make gains in pluralistic political systems. . . . In a pluralist culture, in which different segments of the population profoundly disagree about fundamental goals and values, co-optation would seem to be the optimal way in which to recognize, even honor, minority points of view while maintaining some semblance of *national* solidarity."[34] If co-optation is a diabolical plot of the system, the politics of civility is rightly to be feared. A self-styled, libertarian communist sums it up:

> I am suggesting the need for redistribution and reorganization of power relations in all these institutions with huge popular participation. I am against parties that control governments by means of representative democracy. I want direct democracy in which representatives are recallable at any time and serve limited terms on a rotating basis. *Although the ruling class can co-opt issues, it cannot co-opt control*—that is, the participatory control of the people. Organized radical groups can educate people and participate in their battles for democracy, but cannot claim leadership of popular movements without falling into the mire of elitism.[35]

Technologists and antitechnologists are rightly concerned with the social consequences of technology. Their fear of civil politics is also quite logical. They fear this politics because it stands in the way of utopia and because, all criticism notwithstanding, it is a more viable means of making public policy in complex pluralistic societies than either technocracy or participatory democracy.

Perhaps I am stating the obvious. But I suspect that the fundamentals of civil politics are alien to technologists and antitechnologists alike as they seek to cope with the political environment. They are unwilling to concede that no social order can be a perfect order—a recognition that, I believe, is the mark of political maturity. Modern pluralistic societies are as unlikely to march to the geometric Q.E.D. of politically immature technocrats as to the euphoric Q.E.D. of politically immature libertarians. What stands in their way is the politics of civility.

4 POLITICS AND EDUCATION: THE LONG VIEW AND THE SHORT

Some years ago, reviewing the contemporary state of political science, I noted that "political scientists are riding off in many directions, evidently on the assumption that if you don't know where you are going, any road will take you there."[1] I am very glad, therefore, that we—both students of politics and students of education—have this opportunity to consider the relationship between our respective disciplines and to explore common grounds before we rush off our separate ways doing all kinds of things we should not be doing and neglecting things that we should attend to.

No political scientist who has ever smelled the scent of utopia can escape a fascination with education, and for once, I think, we are not riding off because something is fad or fashion. To believe otherwise would be taking a very short view indeed. And if one were only to take the short view, one would deprive oneself of the sustained efforts made through the centuries by political philosophers to understand the relationship between politics and education.

But if one took only the long view, the result would be stultifying because one would inevitably come to the conclusion of *toujours la même chose*. If the short view is short, the long view, paradoxically, is even shorter. I propose to tread in-between, partly because by education and inclination I have a historical bent of mind, partly because by trained incapacity I cannot ignore the shape of things as they are. Happily, history has always meant to me the study of how things have come to be what they are, so that I have always succeeded in eluding the comfortable assumption either that the past is full of infinite wisdom or that present trends will continue indefinitely into the future.

Let me begin, therefore, at the beginning. The trouble is, of course, that political scientists not only may not know where they are going but also may be in disagreement on where they come from. As I wrote at the earlier occasion, "whether one prefers to trace political science back to Plato and Aristotle, or to the more empirically-minded Machiavelli, or to the establishment of independent academic departments of political science in the late nineteenth century, or to Charles Merriam's *New Aspects of Politics* (1925), is largely a matter of taste."[2] Fortunately, the challenge of this opportunity leads me to amend the statement. Where one begins is perhaps not a matter of taste after all but dictated by what one is interested in. And if one is interested in politics and education, one better begin with Plato and go from there.

What makes Plato so pregnant with meaning today is the current impasse over the relationship between the educational system and the political order. There are those who, because they believe that education is dominated in any case by something they call the military-industrial-political complex, would make the schools staging areas of reform or revolution. And there are those who, because they mistake their establishment views and values for universal verities, would rather throttle education or choke it to death than have it sullied by political reality. Both sides, I suggest, might find it profitable to read Plato. For Plato's *Republic,* it seems to me, represents this myopic view of the relationship between politics and education; in fact, it is *the* educational institution. There is simply no difference between the state of the Republic and its educational system. They are the same because they have the same goal—the well-being of the state. Education is not an end but the means by which human nature can be shaped in the right direction to produce the harmonious state. As the virtuous citizen can only fulfill himself in the *polis,* the state must see to it that training of the young is consonant with the welfare of the state. If the educational system is good, almost any improvement is possible in the political order.

There are two things to be derived by implication from this mini-presentation of Plato on education. First, there is the utopian scent—education can create the perfect political order. And second, because the image of the political order is perfect, at least in the beholder's mind, education can be nothing but the handmaiden of politics. Both presumptions, I daresay, are still very much with us—in whatever guise. They explain, I think, both the optimism and dogmatism of all those, whether of the Right, Center or Left, who believe that if something is wrong with the social and political order, all that is needed to rectify things is more education, better education and morally right education. But, as I said, these are only presumptions, and a presumption is, by definition, a conclusion that is not based on evidence.

Let me put it differently. I know of no political order in the real world which, even if we could agree on its being close to perfection, has been created out of or by an educational system. If anything, the relationship between politics and education, it seems to me, is the other way around. If the political order is sound, stable, legitimate, just, or whatever other criterion of "goodness" one wishes to apply, education and all that is implied by education, such as the creation of new knowledge or the transmission of traditional knowledge, flourishes. If the political order is in trouble, education is in trouble. If we were to follow Plato, or for that matter, Aristotle who believed that education is prior to politics, we would have to conclude that our public troubles—the war in Vietnam, poverty in the ghettos, pollution of the life space, and so on—are due to our educational system. Of course, John Dewey and Dr. Benjamin Spock have been blamed; but I seriously doubt we can take such scapegoating seriously. On the contrary, therefore, if we find our educational system wanting, I think we should try to look at the public order rather than, as we have done so much in education, contemplate our navels as if the outside world did not exist.

Perhaps I am overstating the anticlassical view somewhat, but I do so only because I sense the spell of Plato and Aristotle is still so very much with us, even though it is camouflaged these days in the rhetoric of Herbert Marcuse or the aphorisms of Chairman Mao, on the Left, and the "public philosophy" of Walter Lippmann or the homilies of Max Rafferty, on the Right. But if we assume that it is the political process and the condition of political affairs that make education what it is, I think we find ourselves at the interstices of polity and educational system where political science as a theoretical science and education as an applied science can truly meet on empirical ground.

Let me state all this more formally. I think we have to think of politics, broadly conceived as including both government and societal happenings, as the independent variable and of education as the dependent variable. Now, what bothers me about most of the recent research in political science that deals with education or education-related topics like socialization or attitude formation is that it has been largely cast in the teleological model that is implicit in Plato's and Aristotle's conceptions of the polity. Let me single out as an example *The Civic Culture,* not because it is unique, but because it is undoubtedly the most majestic work of this genre of research.[3] Almond and Verba discover nine relationships between level of education as the independent variable and a variety of political perceptions, attitudes, and behavioral manifestations as the dependent variables. They conclude that "educational attainment appears to have the most important demographic effect on political attitudes."[4] I have no doubt that these relationships exist. But I believe that one or another mix of all the variables subsumed under what is called political culture—whether parochial, participant, subject, or civic—is nothing but one huge tautology that, like Plato's *Republic,* so completely absorbs politics into education and education into politics that explanation of the relationship between politics and education is foreclosed. What is involved is, of course, more than formal education which, Almond and Verba point out, "may not adequately substitute for time in the creation of these other components of the civic culture."[5] But in their subsequent discussion, the Platonic-Aristotelian model (which is basically a teleological and practically an engineering approach) implicit in their premises and inferences is made quite explicit: "The problem, then, is to develop, along with the participation skills that schools and other socializing agencies can foster, affective commitment to the political system and a sense of political community."[6] Now, these are not the words of Plato and Aristotle, but their spirit is there. The good society will emerge if, through proper socializing and educational procedures, in whatever channels and by whatever agents, the right components of the political culture are harnessed in the right direction.[7]

The belief in the omnipotence of education in shaping the political order is reflected in much of the literature on political development. "The educational preparation of at least sizeable segments of a population," writes Robert E. Ward, "is a basic factor in the modernization of political cultures."[8] I find all of these writings troublesome because the formulation of the problem strikes me as eminently circular. For, it seems to me, the introduction of a sophisticated educational system is an *act* of modernization and can, therefore, not be its cause. In many underdeveloped nations which mobilize educationally there are, indeed, effects on the political order, but not necessarily effects that are conducive to a viable politics. The overproduction of high school and college graduates who cannot find meaningful employment often makes for disorder rather than order, but the resultant revolutionary regimes cannot solve the problems that brought them into being. Although an educated elite reinforce traditional status values or special privileges and, at the same time, betray a sense of insecurity as a result of the new education, the political process suffers. "Hence the paradox," writes Lucian Pye of Burma,

> that is the common tragedy for so many underdeveloped countries: those who have been exposed to modern forms of knowledge are often precisely the ones who are most anxious to obstruct the continued diffusion of the effects of that knowledge; they desperately need to hold on to what they have and avoid all risks. The lasting consequence of their formal education has thus been an inflexible and conservative cast of mind. Modernization has bred opposition to change.[9]

Not all students of development follow the Aristotelian lead. Holt and Turner, for instance, posit the primacy of government. Referring to the government's participation in modernization, they point out that "during the take-off stage, however, the government became much more involved in the enculturation process through its contribution to and regulation of education, especially at the elementary level."[10] Political development in England, for instance, took place prior to educational development.

My point in all this is merely to suggest that a model that postulates the primacy of politics in the relationship with education may be more appropriate than the classical approach, and the underdeveloped nations certainly offer a rich field for testing relevant hypotheses.

Fortunately, modern political philosophy gives us an alternate to the classical model. But this brings us quickly into the nineteenth century. Hobbes, as far as I can make out, is silent on education, and Locke, though concerned with it, significantly did not see it as a function of education to develop in citizens a sense of civic duty—quite logically, I think, because in his view ideas solely stem from one's own perceptions and can therefore not be subjected to an authority other than that of the person himself. I do not want to dwell on Kant who, insisting on man being treated as an end rather than as a means, is probably Plato's most distinguished antagonist; but the American tradition was barely influenced by him. I shall turn, therefore, to John Stuart Mill's *On Liberty*.

Mill's conception of education flows from the premise that, given the great variety of opinions on questions of value, moral training must leave room for error. Although one opinion may be dominant, the expression of contrary opinions is necessary and desirable because the dominant opinion may turn out to be partial, false, or even dangerous. *On Liberty* was written before universal education, which Mill favored, had been introduced. "If the government would make up its mind to require for every child a good education," he wrote, "it might save itself the trouble of providing one." Implicit in this statement is an interesting distinction between "State education" and the "enforcement of education by the State." Arguments against the former, he believed do not apply to the latter "but to the State's taking upon itself to direct that education, which is a totally different thing." And why did Mill reject "State education?" Let me quote him, for this view is so very different from the Platonic-Aristotelian conception:

> All that has been said of the importance of individuality of character, and diversity in opinions and modes of conduct, involves, as of the same unspeakable importance, diversity of education. A general State education is a mere contrivance for moulding people to be exactly like one another: and as the mould in which it casts them is that which pleases the predominant power in the government, whether this be a monarch, a priesthood, an aristocracy, or the majority of the existing generation; in proportion as it is efficient and successful, it establishes a despotism over the mind, leading by natural tendency to one over the body.[11]

I need not linger over the fact that the times have passed Mill by. Rather, I find his position remarkable for two reasons. First, if I do have to smell the scent of utopia, I find Mill's version much more attractive and congenial than Plato's, for reasons that should be self-evident. But, second, just as the Platonic-Aristotelian conception provides the latent premises for the model of empirical research that takes education as the independent variable, so Mill provides the premises. I think, for any model that takes it as the dependent variable. Almost a hundred years after *On Liberty* was published, another eminent English political theorist and scholar, Ernest Barker, echoes Mill to the effect that "the field of education . . . is not, and never can be, a monopoly of the State." And he gives a reason: "Educational associations—of parents, of teachers, of workers, and of members of religious confessions—are all concerned in the development of educational experiments, and in offering that liberty of choice among types of school and forms of instruction which is essential to the growth of personal and individual capacity.''[12]

What I want to bring out, simply, is what we all know but rarely articulate as specifically as we might; namely, that our value bias is an important criterion in the specification of what we study and how we study it. Our research designs are not neutral by nature, but by articulating and guarding against our value biases, we can at least hope to neutralize them as long as we do our research. It seems to me that there is a profound difference between a research design that takes education (or related processes, such as socialization, indoctrination, propaganda, conditioning, and so on) as the independent variable and a design which takes it as the dependent variable. For if we start from the other end, I think we have a much richer area of investigation opening up before us. And this, I think, is what we mean when we speak of ''politics of education'' as a field of inquiry.

I do not know why the field has been neglected for so many years; why, in fact, there has never been a consistent effort to continue the research on ''civic training'' that Charles E. Merriam organized and directed in the late twenties. There were eight country studies and Merriam's own *The Making of Citizens*. Each study, Merriam reported, was given wide latitude, but each collaborator was enjoined ''(1) that as a minimum there would be included in each volume an examination of the social bases of political cohesion and (2) that the various mechanisms of civic education would be adequately discussed.''[13] Among these mechanisms, Merriam continued,

> are those of the schools, the role of governmental services and officials, the place of political parties, and the function of special patriotic organizations; or, from another point of view, the use of traditions in building up civic cohesion, the place of political symbolism, the relation of language, literature, and the press, to civic education, the position occupied by locality in the construction of a political loyalty; and, finally, it is hoped that an effective analysis may be made of competing group loyalties rivaling the state either within or without.[14]

In his later *Systematic Politics,* Merriam emphasized that ''the struggle for the schools is almost as significant as that for the control of the army, perhaps more important in the long run. . . . We may merely note that some of the most vital of the power problems center in processes often only remotely associated with the grimmer realities of conventionalized authority.''[15]

There is certainly something of the prophetic in Merriam's appraisal. We surely witness today a struggle over our educational institutions unmatched in history. Unfortunately, empirical political science has little to contribute to either an understanding of the conflict over the control of education or to possible solutions (though I suspect we may have to learn to live with unsolved problems for a long time to come). I must plead a good deal of ignorance in the matter, but as I search through my library I find only a few items that, in one way or another, meet Merriam's challenge to investigation. If one leaves out the burgeoning literature on political socialization and related topics which, I argued, is really inspired by the education-as-independent-variable model, I can think only of such works as *State Politics and the Public School,* by Masters, Salisbury, and Eliot;[16] of *The Political Life of American Teachers,* by Harmon Zeigler;[17] and of the stimulating, if "soft," *The Public Vocational University: Captive Knowledge and Public Power,* by Edgar Litt.[18] And I don't think the situation in political sociology is much better. There are, undoubtedly, case studies of local situations (as in Dahl's *Who Governs?*), but a systematic, empirical body of knowledge on the politics of education does not exist.

I hope very much that this workshop will generate enough research ideas to remedy the situation. Just to be constructive, let me put in some input.

1. Instead of doing so much work on political socialization, we might ask how the rapid circulation of political elites in America influences the educational system. How is the educational system affected by the conditions of political recruitment and turnover in personnel among those who control it? Are some of the troubles besetting the schools due to the volatility of recruitment processes?

2. How is the educational system affected by the existence of individual differences in intellectual interest and capacity, on the one hand, and government policies to provide equal opportunities for education, on the other hand? How can the educational system be "calibrated" to meet the variety of societal needs for different jobs—from janitors and unskilled workmen to Supreme Court Justices? What are the political implications of "manpower manipulation" through education?

3. Why is it that the "educational lobby" is relatively weak? Who are the "natural" allies of education in the determination of national, state, or local educational policies? Would education be better off, or would it be worse off, if it were "taken out" of politics or politics were taken out of education? Why do most interest groups other than those directly involved in education not see the stakes they have in education?

4. What are the consequences of centralization and decentralization of control structures for education? Although this has been much debated, I don't think there is much reliable evidence. Cross-national comparisons are indicated.

5. What are the effects on education of the continuing efforts on the part of those who would use educational institutions to achieve their own political ends? How can education resist the encroachment of outside interests, be they rightist-oriented legislative inquiries or leftist-inspired movements? How can the school be a "laboratory of democracy" and yet remain sufficiently autonomous not to become, as in the Soviet Union, an instrument of the garrison state?

6. In treating the school itself as a "political system," we must surely ask questions about the balance between authority and liberty that is conducive to education; in short, reconceptualizing the school as a political system cannot avoid the old controversy over "discipline." How true is the progressive notion that too much (what is "too much?") discipline makes for aggression which is the enemy of tolerance and corresponding guilt which is the enemy of political responsibility? (To judge from the current generation, presumably brought up in a relaxed manner, there is even more aggression and guilt.)

Let me leave it at that. Let me also reemphasize that my premise, throughout, has been the Millian view of the individual as the goal of all educational effort. This is, of course, both a normative and an utopian premise. As I see the excesses now being perpetrated on our high school and college campuses in the name of freedom, I am by no means sure that this premise is viable. But, I think, it is a premise worth defending. Perhaps it is up to government to protect the schools against their own excesses; which is, I posit, a nice twist on John Stuart Mill. But such must be the view of a latter-day liberal who, unlike conservative and radical, does not see in government the source of all evil.[19]

POLITICAL NORMS IN EDUCATIONAL POLICY MAKING

If, as is sometimes said, politics were simply the art of the possible, appraising the political component of options in choice making on public policies and their consequences would be relatively easy. At least it would not be more difficult than assessing options in economic decision making where standards of rational behavior are assumed to guide choice and thus permit reasonably accurate predictions of outcomes. But politics is not only the art of the possible; it is also a labyrinth of intangibles through which decision makers must find their way, often by trial and error, if they wish to promote their own policy objectives or subvert the objectives of their opponents.

PATTERNS OF POLITICAL BEHAVIOR

The culture of politics, unlike that of economics, provides for rules, roles, norms, or standards which often tend to defy ordinary rationality and escape systematic comprehension, yet which in the long run are conducive to the achievement of political goals. To capture these rules or norms—frequently informal understandings—in models of the political process is difficult, but this very difficulty is reason for doubting the viability of the recently proposed models of political process which would treat political decisions as if they were only economic ones.[1]

Because we increasingly speak of the "economics of education" and the "politics of education" in the same breath, it does not follow that the behavioral patterns involved are merely two sides of the same coin. Politics is an arena of action in which the goals of policy making are generally more ambiguous than in economics. In fact, there may be no goals at all, at least at the level of the collectivity, so that politics becomes eminently concerned with goal setting as its primary activity. Examples are the economists' concern with *competition* and the political scientists' concern with *conflict*. Competition is a form of contention that is possible if goals are given or are reasonably clear: the contending parties agree on goals, and this agreement makes competition feasible. Both sides want essentially the same thing; for instance, economic firms compete for consumers and profits. There is, of course, competition in politics as well, as when two democratic parties compete for voter support and public offices. But, more often than not, political contention is conflictual because there is no agreement on goals; and when there is agreement, politics loses much of its luster. Further, where consensus exists, political actors may also entertain hidden agendas that make for tension and new conflicts. But the resolution of such tensions or conflicts may follow paths that need not be political, such as the specification of formal jurisdictions, the invocation of specialized expertise, the circulation of personnel, or the hierarchical determination of issues.

Politics certainly utilizes these pathways of conflict resolution. Especially it does so in decisional contexts which, like those in the Congress and the more modernized state legislatures of California, Illinois, and New York, have become increasingly streamlined as a result of executive influence, party discipline, specialization of labor among committees, and the emergence of professional staffs. But elected politicians, unlike appointed administrators, cannot easily be contained by management practices. Although the norm of seniority, for instance, is a powerful control device, Young Turks are always ready to rebel; although a committee structure based on a functional division of labor may be present, it can be—and often is—circumvented in the assignment of bills by a wily speaker or reference committee; although the party organization may threaten the insurgent with nonsupport at the polls, the rebel's constituency relationships may be good enough to make party discipline an empty threat. Politics is, above all, a collegial game in which conflicts are resolved by strategies of behavior—strategies of bargaining, exchanging, compromising, persuading, and negotiating—that assume power differentials among the players. Let us listen to a Congressman who was asked, "what would happen when the Senate and the House have different views about higher education?" He replied:

The House usually wins. I say that facetiously. We like to think we do. I guess the Senate likes to think it wins and I guess in a conference no one wins. You have to finally subordinate your views. No one can lose, no one can win. There have to be compromises. Senators, because of the size of their constituency and because of the diversity of the areas that they must cover in their Senatorial sevice, usually can't be expected to be informed on the details of these programs as can House members who have . . . smaller constituencies and less demands upon their legislative time to do a great, wide range of things. So most House members, not all, but most become more highly specialized in the particular area that they work in. And when you get in conference that begins to show up. The Senate has to rely on staff to make decisions. House members usually rely more upon their own expertise than the Senators. It is just the nature of the institutions as much as anything else. But really no one side wins all the time. I think the Senate is usually pretty generous in accommodating the House in its requests, but it is based on that understanding that House members do have an opportunity to see more of the details of the operation or programs than does a Senator, and I find that true in most conferences. While Senators will stick tenaciously to good things they believe in, they do recognize that there is a difference in the way we approach problems. No reflection on them at all. A Senator has got to be a great generalist and he has to place great reliance upon his staff, because he has just got too many decisions to make, while we are confined to narrower fields, comparatively speaking.

There is, of course, coercion as well, but it is a strategy that politicians risk only if the payoff will likely be greater than the price of retaliation. It rarely is. Politicians are past masters in the fine art of decisional cost accounting. Partisanship as a hidden form of coercion will be avoided by the clever politician. A congressional committee chairman is speaking:

I simply never have been as partisan as some of my Democratic friends. I know that they disapprove of this. They do not like it and criticize me for it. But it seems to me that in regard to long-range goals you must have bipartisan support, and it just makes no sense to do otherwise. And I frankly think that Congressman X is just as much interested in good education at the college and university level as I am, and he's got a lot of good ideas, and it is pretty sad not to bring it out on the floor without the bipartisan support; so I just stay in the committee and don't try to get the bill to a vote until we have that.

The impact of political norms, standards, or criteria conducive to conflict resolution on choice of policy alternatives and assessment of consequences is difficult to harness in a model of the political process that links content of policies with decision-making procedures. The parties interested in educational policy making—educational associations, lobbies, college and university administrators, faculty, and even students and their parents—are likely to see the educational arena as more or less self-contained. For politicians, however, education is only one item on the agenda of issues that call for the specification of goals and the setting of priorities. Within education itself the field of higher education is only one component. The politician's frame of reference is necessarily larger than that of any particular interest, and he cannot afford to neglect a variety of interests that may be germane to his political needs. As a result, the politician is involved in a complex maze of negotiations over diverse political issues. A Republican U.S. Senator from a Mountain state expressed this sensitivity to the play of interests in the educational field alone:

The higher education interest groups obviously are diverse. They also have an internecine warfare going on between them which is sometimes very extraordinary. Generally speaking, people think of the Catholics, for example, as being more or less monolithic in their efforts to promote a certain type of educational support. As a matter of fact, they are not. There are about four different groups in the Catholic educational process, and they are fighting between themselves, but they only have one spokesman here, and he is for the group that is militant and trying to get aid. There is a group of people in the Catholic educational field who don't want it or want it in a different form. Then you have the problems of the land-grant colleges versus the state-supported institutions which are not land-grant. Land-grant colleges, by and large, want to have the only direct aid of anybody in the educational field. And then, of course, you have the public-supported universities versus the private institutions, but this is not as extreme as I thought it might be. It was very bitter for a while between the public schools and the Catholics in particular. I find, however, that you also have problems with the Lutheran schools, you have problems with some of the Jewish, and I am sure we have problems with some of the Episcopalians, although they are not quite as vocal about it. . . . Therefore, on the whole, we recognize on the committee, I think, that there isn't one educational bloc as such, although they all want to get more funds. That's about the only thing they really agree on.

In order to protect himself from undue exposure to pressures and commitments in any one area of public policy that may get him into trouble in another area, the politician has invented standards of choice and norms of conduct that serve this purpose. He jealously safeguards his freedom of action. The political requirements of being involved in a host of policy arenas call for strategies that make the political process appear kaleidoscopic, diffuse, and intangible. These strategies and accompanying norms have the effect of making politicians appear men of virtue somewhat less than most of them probably are. The American politician suffers from occupational role strains that make his status more ambivalent than that of most professionals.[2]

Much has been written about the roles that politicians play in legislating public policies and representing their constituencies,[3] the styles of response they adopt vis-à-vis interest and pressure groups,[4] the norms by which they regulate their conduct toward each other,[5] the informal relationships that bind them together,[6] the strategies they follow in seeking to obtain their objectives,[7] and the significance they ascribe to expertise in the making of decisions.[8] But these studies have dealt with the behavioral patterns involved either in general terms (independent of particular policy arenas) or (at the other extreme) in the context of specific case studies of low generalizability.[9] Even if these patterns and their consequences for public policy making are sufficiently irregular to make lawlike generalizations difficult, they are not as random as the case studies in particular arenas of public policy seem to suggest.

Unfortunately, studies that connect patterns of political behavior, including standards of choice and norms of conduct, to broad areas of public policy rather than to specific instances (say, trade legislation or defense appropriations) are rare. In the field of educational policy they are even rarer, and in the field of higher education they are almost nonexistent.[10] One may speculate about the impact of political norms on the content of public policies and their implications for policy making in higher education, yet the speculation would probably only obfuscate what is likely to be the case. I shall limit myself in what follows, therefore, to some limited findings of a survey of American state politicians, chiefly legislators but also some executives. These findings fall somewhere between general statements that might fit the educational arena and the recitation of instances in which political standards or norms affected the choice among policy options and possibly their consequences.

NATURE OF THE SURVEY

In 1968 I was commissioned by the Carnegie Commission on Higher Education to survey how state legislators and certain state executive officials perceived the problems and issues of higher education, their attitudes towards various aspects of higher education, and their expectations of future developments.[11] As a result, we conducted fairly intensive, mainly taped interviews with a highly selected group of respondents in California, Texas, Illinois, New York, Pennsylvania, Iowa, Kansas, Kentucky, and Louisiana.[12] These states were selected because they are located in different regions of the country and are characterized by various complex systems of higher education. The respondents, about twelve in each state, were selected for their importance in policy making in higher education, such as speakers, floor leaders, or chairmen of education and finance committees. Fifty-six respondents were Democrats and forty-six were Republicans. The limited, but by no means arbitrary, nature of the sample precluded making exact distributive statements. We were interested in discovering qualities of expression and themes. Although none of our open-end questions was designed to probe for standards of choice or norms of conduct, observations with regard to at least some of them can be made. In particular, I shall deal here with four norms that emerged most strongly from the interview protocols—the norm of responsiveness, the norm of passivity in oversight, the norm of authority, and the norm of comparison. I shall, in conclusion, deal with the respondents' reactions to the central question of the theme, "Higher Education for Everybody?"

THE NORM OF RESPONSIVENESS

Politicians are prone to protest that their policy positions are dictated by "conscience," by their convictions of what is right or wrong. But the luxury of this role orientation is readily sacrificed if constituency pressures are sufficiently strong to preclude the consideration of alternatives. In the latter case, the norm of independent judgment is readily displaced by the norm of responsiveness, which is probably the norm taken more seriously by politicians themselves as well as by their publics. Yet, this norm seems to be of limited relevance in policy making concerning higher education because constituency opinion (rather than constituency interest, which may or may not be articulated) is of relatively low political salience most of the time. Of course, constituency silence may be due to the politician's ability to anticipate reactions to what he might do, and this "law of anticipated reactions'' makes it difficult to trace the flow of cause and effect in the educational policy-making process.

Our evidence suggests that the public does not communicate much with state politicians concerning higher education and that such exchange as occurs tends to be sporadic and unorganized, usually dealing with some specific matter but not with higher education as an institutional concern of society. A respondent confirmed the lack of interest in higher education policies on the part of the general public:

> INTERVIEWER: We are asking you all these questions because we know that legislators hear a good deal about education from their constituents and interest groups. From whom in your district are you most likely to hear about higher education?

> RESPONDENT: Well, that's a false assumption. We hear from the voters only about the [secondary] schools, damn near don't hear from anybody about higher education. The only time I can think of we've heard anything much was when the new campuses were proposed, and that was mainly not from people in my district, but from the private institutions and from some people who had an interest in getting the campus one place or another. But that's very unusual.

When legislators do hear from constituents, it is rarely from the average citizen. Respondents almost unanimously reported that most of their contacts at home, if there are contacts, are with people directly connected with the colleges and universities. A Texas legislator with a junior college and a respected private university in his district reported:

> We never hear anything from ordinary citizens about higher education. I never have. I have never gotten a single letter from a single constituent asking me for an opinion about anything in higher education.

A member of the Illinois House Appropriations Committee indicated a similar paucity of correspondence:

> I would say that 95 percent of my correspondence or communications from my district on education deals with grammar schools and high schools, not with higher education—although I think in my district a very high percentage of people do go to college.

The reason for popular silence, in respondents' views, is simple enough—people outside the field of higher education simply do not think about it. As a result, some politicians equate constituent silence with satisfaction. A Louisiana respondent expressed this position well, as follows:

> Well, I think that the parents are well satisfied, so there are no real comments or bad comments. Their children are getting into the schools they want to go to; we've been accepting them. So, I don't think they're aware of the real problems

in education—whether we're getting the proper education or whether our dollar is being spent properly. . . . They see their child go through school, they see see him graduate, and they're pleased; and so there's not much comment. They're satisfied.

A New Yorker said very much the same thing:

Very few members of the public have the slightest knowledge of what is going on. The mother and father are concerned about whether their son is going to get into college; that is what they are concerned about. As long as you are making that available, and you are making it possible for them economically, that's it.

Unfortunately, our interviews were conducted prior to the disorders at Columbia University in the spring of 1968 and the subsequent escalation of student unrest throughout the country. Recent events in Congress and some state legislatures have shown that campus disorders do have an impact on legislative policy making in higher education. An Iowa respondent, who thought it was "appalling how little people really worry" about higher education as such, described the kinds of things that stimulate constituent complaints and, presumably, legislative response:

They are concerned when the students burn their draft cards, when kids take the law into their own hands, and a few get out of line. Some of them are upset about hippies and a few about the kind of kookie fellows and kookie professors who get into the press. But they aren't, I'm afraid, concerned with higher education as such.

Yet, if complaints do occur and the mail is heavy, legislators are not necessarily impressed. "Just because you get a pile of letters doesn't mean that everybody is thinking that way," a Californian stated; and invoking the norm of responsiveness, he continued: "It's the people that aren't writing to you—you have to evaluate their attitudes too." And another respondent argued:

You hear usually from people who do not have a four-year institutional experience. They are only reacting against the use of four-letter words. . . . These are people who are religiously oriented, and they object to the taxpayers' dollars being spent for things they don't believe in.

These and similar remarks reflect what is well known about a politician's response to communications and pressure. If what he hears agrees with his views, even if it comes from a minority, his response will be favorable; if what he hears disagrees with his views, his response tends to be unfavorable. His own freedom of action depends on the balancing of diverse viewpoints that he can discern, but the norm of responsiveness is likely to be invoked only if it suits his predispositions or if he feels threatened at the polls.

Higher education, it appears, has low salience in the perceptual world of state politicians because the conditions of high salience—articulated demands from a broad section of the electorate or from highly intense special interests—are missing. As a result, the average legislator is likely to give his attention to other matters that loom more prominently in his mind as he sets his own legislative priorities. While this indifference deprives the legislature of significant inputs, it frees higher education of some political constraints that might otherwise be present. Higher education policies or appropriations are less likely to be subject to the kind of bargaining that takes place in policy areas where the stakes are seen as significant for political survival, especially for politicians from districts that are highly competitive in either primaries or general elections.[13]

THE NORM OF PASSIVITY IN OVERSIGHT

Oversight of administration is generally accepted as a legitimate function of legislative bodies. This function is difficult to distinguish from control, but the distinction does not matter here because, whether oversight or control, the behavioral patterns, as far as higher education is concerned, appear to be dominated by a norm of passivity. Nor does it matter whether the norm is deliberate or itself the consequence of other circumstances in the legislature's environment. Most legislators in the nine states of the survey felt that legislative oversight should be limited to the most general budgetary matters and to the broadest policy guidelines. For instance, the particulars of admission, curriculum, and even construction are considered essentially "academic affairs" best left to executive supervision or to the institutions themselves. A California assemblyman made the point:

> If you start controlling the curriculum you control the end product. I'd sort of back away from that. I think that . . . the Legislature should determine to what extent it wants to finance specialized kinds of education in the professional areas and law schools, medical schools, and that sort of thing. But it should be on a basis of evaluating recommendations made by the institutions themselves and by the Coordinating Council itself. I think the initiative ought to come there. And we have to evaluate these in terms of our set of priorities. What we can afford and what we can't afford.

When the norm of passivity is rationalized, it seems to derive either from a belief that "academic freedom" should be protected by legislative self-restraint and that "politics" should be kept out of higher education or from a realization that legislators are not really qualified to make decisions on matters that call for "professional" determination. In part this deference to professionalism in higher education seems to stem from a profound sense of reality. Legislators recognize that their environment is characterized by too much work, too little time, and not enough staff to permit more than perfunctory attention to the oversight function.

Like all norms, of course, the norm of passivity may be broken. At least some respondents revealed that the legislature does not always follow the principle of nonintervention in academic affairs. Instances of legislative retaliation against university officials who, in the legislators' judgment, are reluctant to control student unrest and radical activities were cited as examples of situations in which the legislature had been "forced to act" because professional university administrators were neglecting their responsibilities to the best interests of the state's taxpayers. Our respondent put it this way:

> I generally subscribe to the view of autonomy as far as the academic community is concerned, and I feel that we must rely on the people in education to make the decisions which affect education. That's about the best answer that I can give you, and I've tended to oppose efforts to use the pursestrings to force the academic community into courses of action which it was reluctant to take. I do think, though, autonomy means responsibility and I think that if higher education doesn't function responsibly and doesn't deal with these problems in a way which satisfies the public, which convinces the public that it's getting its so-called taxpayer dollar's worth, then there will be pressure on the legislature to involve itself in higher education.

In general, it appears, passivity in oversight is the norm in the state legislature's stance toward higher education. This self-restraint on the legislature's part is probably conducive to academic self-determination. In the view of some legislators, the norm is broken if the institutions of higher learning act "irresponsibly." The stress that legislators are inclined to place on being "forced to act" under certain conditions is perhaps the best proof of the norm's significance. They evidently prefer quiescence to turbulence in their relationships with the academic community.

THE NORM OF AUTHORITY

Closely related to, and in some respects a corollary of, the norm of passivity is the norm of authority. In many state legislatures, specialization is highly institutionalized so that effective decision making, in contrast to formal voting, is in the hands of individuals who occupy the crucial gatekeeping positions in the legislative hierarchy—particularly chairmen and senior members of committees or subcommittees. Not only are these gatekeepers of the legislative business the best informed on matters of higher education, but also the flow of communication to the legislature as a whole seems to cease at this point of the decision-making process. The small amount of information on higher education matters available to the rank and file in turn induces them to depend on the recommendations of those in the know. The norm of authority emerges as an important variable affecting educational policy decisions. A California legislative leader stated the predicament of the rank and file as follows:

> Let me put it this way. I'm a senior member of the Senate. I'm now in the upper quarter of the men here on the basis of seniority, so I'm put into committees

where the needs become more obvious to me. But to the men who are not, I
think they have real voids [in information]. The men who have never served
on the Education or Finance Committee, that's the majority of the Senate, I don't
think they know enough about [higher education]. I don't think it's brought to
them enough.

The rank-and-file perspective was articulated in detail by this respondent:

The budget as originally prepared at the department level doesn't have any
possible way of getting to us. . . . We hardly have any idea of what it was in
the beginning. What did some professor or some department head have in mind
when he was preparing his budget perhaps eighteen months or two years before
the document ever arrives to us? What really are the desires and the ambitions
and the plans of the people down at the department levels in these various
schools? Surely, somebody has some imagination; somebody is offering some
dramatic new programs. These things are all weeded out before we ever get them.

Asked if there were some way to change the situation, he continued:

We seem to be enmeshed in the established bureaucracy. The bureaucracy works
fairly well, but it does seem to make the transmission of information between the
legislators and the people out in the field difficult. I don't know . . . I just feel
frustration that the lines of communication are so long and they have so many
obstacles. It is very difficult to see the real picture if you have to get it after
all these siftings.

Although most rank-and-file members of the legislature probably share this
respondent's predicament, most have learned to live with it. Not surprisingly,
therefore, most legislators want guidance from, and are prepared to accept the
authority of, their colleagues who are on the inside of policy making concerning
higher education, and they are willing to rely on the recommendations that come
from the governor or special administrative bodies such as boards of regents or
coordinating councils. Indeed, there appears to be a general feeling that these
agencies, rather than the legislature, should be the primary governmental force in
the state's system of higher education. Reliance on the authority of expertise may
at times be resented, but it is a norm of conduct that under modern conditions of
specialization cannot be readily dispensed with.

THE NORM OF COMPARISON

A Supreme Court justice once referred to the American states as "experimental chambers," suggesting that innovative policies might be tried in one state
and, if successful, imitated in other states, and failure in one state would not have
dire consequences in others. The evidence from our study is overwhelming that
legislators pay close attention to what is happening to higher education in other

states. The norm of comparison appears to be well institutionalized and to affect educational decisions.

Although most legislators, in making comparisons between their own state's system of higher education and that of other states, tended to view their own in a favorable light, they discriminated among the states which serve as standards of comparison. Legislators in California and New York most often compared each other's systems; they seemed to agree that the New York schools were rapidly approaching the excellence of California schools. Needless to say, the New Yorkers were pleased, while the Californians were concerned. According to a New Yorker:

> Yes, we make that comparison with California all the time. . . . during the whole debate in the early sixties, the question of California and New York came up. . . . I think we are keeping up with them. We weren't for a long time, but we are now.

On the other hand, California respondents admitted that their state was losing ground to New York. For instance:

> I think we're number one, but New York is catching up with us. In the next five years we will be number two. . . . I don't think the Senate knows how fast New York is moving. . . . At the rate we're going, we will not be able to keep up. We're going to have to be cutting back. Instead of talking about growing in California with population demands, we are talking about back-paddling.

Legislators in the other relatively wealthy states—Illinois, Texas, and Pennsylvania—also paid heed to New York or California. An Illinois official stated, for instance:

> We look at the leading states of the nation—the large states, the wealthy states, the industrial states—with which to make our comparisons. . . . We ask if Illinois is doing as much as California. . . . We don't compare with other states. We don't use national norms to make our comparisons. Except if we fall below them, we feel that we really are behind because we should be far ahead of the national norms.

Although respondents in states with educationally less developed systems also often cited California or New York as models, they tended to make comparisons with states that were similar to their own in the level of development of higher education or of economic wealth, or that were geographically propinquitous. In doing so, many different criteria of "relative indulgence" or "relative deprivation" served the purposes of comparison. A Kentucky respondent, for instance, applied the yardstick of economic capability:

> Now, from my knowledge of what exists in other states and Kentucky, I don't know of any area that we're lagging behind in higher education. Oh, true, we could

pick out some states with heavily endowed colleges and that sort of thing, and some states with heavier taxes, such as California, that are perhaps doing more than Kentucky as far as ability to pay goes, than Kentucky is doing. Certainly, for a state like Kentucky, not the richest of the states by any means, we're making, I think, maximum effort in higher education.

A Texan, making a regional comparison, was

highly pleased. At least as far as with what we would classify as the Southern states or the Southwestern states. . . . I would say that we rank number one.

But another Texas respondent was more sober:

You have to talk about higher education in Texas in two completely different frames of reference—one is the University of Texas at Austin and the other is everybody else. If you talk about Austin, I think you would have to say that we are up with the top ten or fifteen public institutions in the country. Perhaps I am over-optimistic about that, but I get the impression that we are making some very important strides at that institution. If you talk about the rest of them, I think that they are sadly substandard. If you compare them with California, it is just ludicrous. If you compare them with the state university system in New York, it is just—well, there is not any comparison. . . . The basic problem here is that we have too many schools, too little central coordination, and too much politics involved in who gets what.

There can be no question that the norm of comparison is a powerful stimulus in guiding development in higher education, as it is in many other policy areas.[14] Comparing one's own state with others makes for imitation and the diffusion of innovations. The norm of comparison has clearly a significant influence on the policy process as well as policy outcomes in the field of higher education.

HIGHER EDUCATION FOR EVERYBODY?

The norms I have reviewed so far are essentially procedural rules which are especially germane to decision making concerning higher education. What of substantive norms—those basic policy positions on which a broad consensus might be expected to exist or which, on the contrary, may be sources of conflict? It is appropriate, in the context of a conference which seeks to shed light on the question of ''Higher Education for Everybody?'' to conclude with a resume of legislators' orientations in this matter. It is a question on which polity and university may be disagreed. Yet, surprisingly, only relatively few of our hundred-odd respondents supported unequivocally the idea of universal public higher education; many more either rejected it or stated important qualifications.

Endorsement of universal higher education came primarily from legislators in the largest states with complex systems—Texas, California, and New York. In general, universal higher education was seen to benefit state and nation as much as the individual student. A California senator responded enthusiastically to the question "Would you say that everyone is entitled to a college education at public expense?" as follows:

Absolutely, absolutely. I believe that the nation benefits from this. I don't think that everybody would end up going to college because some people are obviously not going to go. But for those who want to go, there should be an opportunity.

A Texan felt that at least a junior college education should be available:

I think that society has gotten sufficiently complex that everybody should be entitled, at this point, to a junior college education. I'm not prepared to say that everybody ought to be entitled to a four-year education.

Most of those favorable to universal higher education stressed that young men and women should have the "opportunity" to go to college, though not neecessarily at public expense: "I will say that I think every student in this state who wants to go to college should have the opportunity. I didn't say free," one respondent put it. Some legislators emphasized that, with opportunity given, the initial responsibility for seeking a higher education should be up to the individual student. For instance:

I said at the beginning that I didn't think the state necessarily should furnish everyone with a college education. I think it's the obligation of the state to furnish every boy and girl an opportunity to get an education. But I think they should do it and must do it on their own initiative.

At times, opportunity was linked to the problem of student ability and desire, as in this response:

Everyone who has the desire and the ability [should be able to go to college]. And the two go together. I think the question of abilities is a very difficult one to solve. Again, it is a mixture of motivation, ability, and previous training. . . . But the area of opportunity lies in higher education in our society. You cannot make it in our society . . . unless you have gone to college.

A few respondents opposed college education for everybody at public expense. Most of them thought it infeasible because of financial problems, and some felt that some young people might simply not be qualified. Others felt that students themselves should contribute to financing their education, on the ground that they would then have more of a stake in it and get more out of it. Loan programs were seen as an alternative to free education. A Pennsylvania official stated:

I would place the burden of repaying on each one who would secure the benefits of higher education. Through that method I think they will get much more out of it. The other day at an educational conference one man spoke up and said he had sweated blood to get a little education on his own and now he's sweating blood to get an education for his boy and girl and he believed that he was wrong—that the boy and girl should be doing their own sweating.

The variety of responses to the question on universal public education, ranging from enthusiastic support to bitter opposition, pinpoints the ambiguity of educational goals. Curiously, ambiguity concerning goals is something that legislative bodies and academic institutions characteristically share. It makes them similar in some respects; yet it is also a continuing source of tensions between them, for goal ambiguity may tend to impede communication. Higher education for everybody may mean a great many different things to different legislators and different academicians.

Higher education is expected to provide a multiplicity of services for society. The university's goals include not only educating undergraduate and professional students, but also giving expert advice to government, doing research for government and private industry or agriculture, training employees for all sorts of business, holding conferences for men of learning as well as for laymen, and participating in their communities' social and economic affairs. In part, this heterogeneity of objectives and activities stems from the university's diverse constituencies, just as the legislature's diversity of positions on all kinds of public issues derives from its diverse constituencies. University administrators, faculty, and students have different conceptions of the mission of higher education; so do governing boards, political officials, private donors to the educational enterprise, and taxpayers in the general public. As a result, decisions affecting higher education, inside the university and outside in the legislature or elsewhere, are all influenced by different participants' own definitions of the role of higher education in society and its relation to other societal or private goals.

When goals are ambiguous, contention over objectives and their instrumentation is likely to be conflictual. Legislatures are, of course, institutions that are partly rooted in conflict and their operations are predicated on the crystallization, clarification, and resolution of conflicts involving both the means and ends of policy. Universities are not generally thought of as political institutions; yet anyone familiar with the internal workings of higher education institutions will probably agree that the conflict model of politics provides a fairly satisfactory fit. When legislatures and universities come into contact, as of necessity they must, the goal ambiguity characteristic of either institution is surely a source of misunderstanding and, possibly, controversy. On the other hand, the very flexibility in policy formulation that goal ambiguity permits is, over the long haul, conducive to the resolution of disagreements and the emergence of a democratic consensus, provided the participants in this political game play by its conventional rules.

6 REASON AND RELEVANCE: ON A MADNESS OF RECENT TIMES

The eighteenth century is rightly known as the Age of Reason. Yet, at the end of the century, during the French Revolution, Reason, now spelled with a capital R, was temporarily enthroned (by at least one Jacobin faction) as the goddess of a new order—a new order that had begun with high hopes for the dignity of man but ended in a reign of terror. Reason was to be the new divinity of a revolution that, at least in the minds of some of its ideologues, had sought human emancipation from the shackles of the divine. Indeed, statues were actually erected for the glory of the new goddess; some of the churches of France reverberated with sermons and litanies that celebrated the new religion. Reason, for the philosophers and scientists of The Enlightenment, had been a tool to cleanse the mind of irrationality and superstition. It was now worshipped as if it had the substance of gold and the face of a Mona Lisa. Unfortunately, not even a great idea can survive when intellectuals adopt the mood of the mob and succumb to the temper of the time.

Analogies are treacherous things. While they may be suggestive, they never explain anything. Yet, I cannot resist the temptation of calling attention to the similarity between the uses made of "Reason" by the extremists of the French Revolution and the uses made of "Relevance" in our own troubled times. That both concepts begin with "r" is, I assume, purely coincidental. But the analogy is not far fetched. "The shouts of 'relevance' that have been cracking our ears for the past half decade," Robert Brustein noted a little while ago, "are now reverberating through the halls of almost every university department, and particularly through the corridors of the social sciences."

What happened in the sixties in the universities, from Tokyo to Cairo, Paris, Berlin, Columbia, Berkeley, and back to Tokyo, was not something especially novel, but the subversion of an idea that has always been an important component of the cluster of ideas about the relationship between science and society, between knowledge and action. How science or knowledge is or can be applied to the problems of society is an old question, but today's students evidently had to rediscover it.

Unfortunately, the agony of rediscovery became a matter of quasi-religious revelation more than a shock of secular recognition. This cannot be the occasion for reviewing the history of the debate over the relationship between knowledge and action that began with Marx's critique of philosophy and has remained unresolved ever since for the simple reason, I suspect, that no solution is possible. That one may have to live with unsolved and possibly unsolvable problems is not something easy to teach or easy to learn. It is a dilemma that we will continue to face and that we will probably find even more difficult to solve in an era of rapid social and technological change. I see no alternative but living with it as best we can.

There are, it seems to me, two ways in which one can deal with the problem of relevance as it has been posed in recent years. First, it seems desirable to expose the anti-intellectualism of the latter-day quest for relevance, at least as it was formulated by some enthusiasts. This I propose to do, if only by way of suggestion, and largely in order to clear the underbrush for a second way of tackling the problem. This second way is to treat the issue of relevance as a serious epistemological problem.

The demand for relevance, though often proclaimed in the name of lofty principles, was essentially vulgar. To put it as simply as possible, it was boorish and anything but iconoclastic. I sometimes wonder what a man like Thorstein Veblen would have said about the things that were perpetrated in the name of relevance in our universities (especially when a professor took a stand on an issue that displeased some students).

Let me quote from a statement made at a conference held at the Center for the Study of Democratic Institutions in August, 1967, to show how perilously close we came to the subversion of academic inquiry. Here is a Berkeley student speaking:

> The way universities are set up now, the whole idea is that a professor is not personally responsible for his ideas—that is to say, it's a free marketplace of ideas and you can't beat up a professor if he has ideas that are obnoxious to you.
>
> That ethic, which in some respects is a very crude one, has led to the attitude that nobody is to be held responsible for what he believes. Professors can say any old nonsense in class and never have to be held accountable. This personifies the tragic disjuncture between thought and action in this country. But what radical politics does is to make people accountable for what they actually believe and what they say; so that for the first time a professor will not only have to give a lecture and say whatever he pleases, he will also have to take a stand on an issue that his students are terribly concerned with at the moment . . .

My purpose is not to belabor the threat implied in making academics responsible for their beliefs. I only want to suggest to what moral position an extremist version of the quest to put knowledge into action in the name of relevance can lead and to summarize some meanings of relevance that have been suggested, explicitly or implicitly, in the recent past.

First, being relevant means to give a simple and immediately comprehensible explanation of what are really very complicated problems. More often that not, the explanation is of the one-factor variety: environmental problems are due to the greed for quick profits; prison problems are due to the guards' brutality; war is due to economic imperialism, etc. Because these matters are urgent, they require immediate solutions; immediate solutions do not permit complicated analysis; complicated analysis is only a pretense for doing nothing.

Second, being relevant means that the content of teaching and research should be as fresh and up-to-date as the morning news broadcast. Treating events historically or philosophically is a cop-out. Living with the puzzles created by new events is, however, intolerable. Attention therefore shifts constantly as new events crowd out old ones. But, as a result, yesterday's good cause is quickly forgotten and today's cause is the only legitimate cause.

Third, being relevant involves entertaining feelings of anger and outrage, and only emotionally satisfying answers rather than empirically tested ones will do. What satisfies feelings is relevant; what satisfies cognitions is not.

Fourth, being relevant means committing oneself and all others, whether they are willing or not, to social and political action. The university should build houses for low-income families, prevent pollution, and exert pressure on government in favor of a preferred reform. The university is a staging area for reform or revolution rather than a place where the mind is cultivated or some skills are learned.

Fifth, being relevant means, at the extreme, that only those who agree with you and are committed to your causes should be heard. Relevance justifies disrupting lectures expressing disliked opinions, preventing interviews with recruiters from what are considered evil institutions, occupying laboratories engaged in research that is disapproved for one reason or another, and finally engaging in violence against persons and property.

Even a Presidential Commission could not resist the call for relevance. Not that the President's Commission on Campus Unrest had much to say in the matter, but what it said was telling. The charge of irrelevance according to the Commission, "comes from students whose presence at the university is not entirely voluntary." The remedy would be, in some cases, "a more voluntary university, with freer entry and exit."

I don't know what to make of this, other than read into it the assumption—an assumption, indeed, articulated by some—that the university resembles a prison. But this is an assumption, or perhaps it is a conclusion, that no reasonably rational person would want to entertain for long. I would think that if a student finds the university not to his liking, he ought to get out and stay out. But this was apparently not a remedy that the Commission dared contemplate.

In other cases, the Commission continued, "the remedy will be a reform of curriculum to include subjects and courses which students find more 'relevant'."

Relevance, in other words, is something that students determine, and teachers are hired hands who give them what they want, evidently on the assumption that students know what they want. This is not an altogether unreasonable assumption, and in my experience as a teacher there have been many students who knew what they wanted. But these students, I daresay, were not the ones who called out for Relevance with a capital R. Rather, it was those who did not know what they wanted who demanded relevance.

The Commission hardly faced up to this reality, and its recommendations, if you read them, are anticlimactic. It closed its remarks on relevance saying that "students demand and deserve an education that will provide them with the knowledge needed to be effective and responsible members of society."

This sounds splendid, but it missed the point. For "to be effective and responsible members of society" was precisely what the devotees of relevance did not care to be. Had the Commission been more imaginative, it might have gone to the curricula of the "free universities," so-called, that mushroomed in the sixties but are now quite dead. The basic maxim of these universities was, I think, that anything that interests anybody is relevant and that anyone can try to organize a course on anything. Courses ranged from Eastern religion to the manufacture of Molotov cocktails, from rock music to the fine art of draft evasion, from the villainy of imperialism to the experience of feel and touch.

What made all of these courses Relevant, with a capital R, was less their subject matter than the simple fact that they were offered by a counter-institution. This circumstance is an important clue to understanding relevance. What, in the context of the counter-institution, was deemed relevant would, if offered by the traditional university, be deemed irrelevant. That this reduction to the political absurd of a term that is of important syntactical use could and would not last is, of course, a matter of hindsight. But there is a lesson to be learned.

Ours is an age that places enormous emphasis on the usefulness of ideas and on practical knowledge. Parochial as we are in thinking about ourselves, we tend to see the problem of practical knowledge as a peculiar trait of Western industrial culture. But in a world of rapid technological change and rapid diffusion of innovations, including political innovations the problem has come to have universal significance.

The question of relevance as a serious matter was perhaps first and most forcefully brought to the attention of the American social science community when, in the late thirties, Robert S. Lynd wrote his book, *Knowledge For What?* The question, as I recall, created something of a shock among students of my generation—a generation, by the way, which would soon occupy many important social-scientific command posts and lesser positions of a nation at war. Lynd's question was an outrageous question, for it raised the issue of the political ends to which knowledge is put. And it was a very dangerous question because it implied that it would be answered politically.

But the two aspects of the question are of a different order. One can say: yes, in the last analysis, all knowledge is put to political ends, insofar as all knowledge contributes, in one way or another, to the human community, and every human community is a political order. It is perfectly sensible, therefore, to ask about the political ends of knowledge.

But it does not follow that the way to answer the question is necessarily a matter of politics or that it should be a matter of politics. For if it were that, then any answer would be a foregone conclusion, and there would be as many answers as there are political views.

However, those who would want to answer the question about the political ends of knowledge in political ways are not inclined to take this tolerant attitude. For they deny that any others but themselves can come to the right answer. In the end, therefore, if the problem of knowledge making were treated as a political problem, those who control the political order would have to impose their views on the rest of society. This is, of course, precisely what continues to happen in political regimes dedicated to the promotion of a single ideology.

As a result of the war, the answer to Robert Lynd's question was put off. As long as one could assume a consensus on political ends, as was the case during the Second World War, the problem of relevance did not arise and the utility of knowledge was assumed to be self-evident.

When, after the war, both physical and social scientists had second thoughts in the matter, political innocence was no longer possible. The post-war debate over the uses of atomic energy was only the most spectacular instance of the new concern.

Most political scientists were prudent and pragmatic. Paradoxically, perhaps, it had been their involvement in wartime government that had sensitized them to the dangers of a politically defined political science.

As post-war social science came to think in terms of probabilities, it also came to acknowledge the limits of what is possible or feasible in the application of its knowledge to public affairs, no matter how desirable certain political goals might be. Being relevant meant that knowledge making involved producing evidence that not only might prove but also falsify an hypothesis.

This understanding of what it means to be relevant in education and research is not the understanding of those who invoke "Relevance" as their battle cry. For relevance has come to be written, just as reason had come to be written in the French Revolution, with a capital R. Relevance is treated as a noun with a substance as Aristotelian as any of that sage's concepts, a substance that is its own justification, a goddess that is worshipped.

If a purely syntactic term is used often enough and feverishly enough, normal pressures for conformity make for belief in its ethical propriety and substantive rationality. Moreover, if in the process of use the term is given a great variety of meanings that, as in the case of relevance, are so subjective that almost anything can be attributed to it, it will have an enormously disorienting effect.

The disorienting effect of relevance deprives us of the minimal sense of inter-subjectivity on which all social relationships, and with them the social nature of knowledge, are necessarily predicated. Ironically, the quest for "knowledge into action" that is so much a part of the Credo of Relevance can have only disastrous consequences for either knowledge or action.

Social action, by which I mean the purposive intervention through human decision in the workings of nature and society, becomes the ultimate justification for the creation of knowledge. *Cogito ergo sum,* dubious as it may be as a formula for orientation, yields to *facio ergo sum*—I act, therefore I am. The end result is the belief that "technological fixes" can remedy all ill-functioning natural and social systems.

The purpose of the technological fix is control or power over some problem—at the moment it is war, poverty, injustice, and pollution. But fixes rarely work as expected. And the presumably relevant body of knowledge comes to be distrusted and, in the minds of some, deserves being destroyed. Smashing the machine goes hand in hand with smashing knowledge.

No reasonable person would want to deny the desirability and need for applying knowledge to the problems of society and its natural environment. This is a truism whose mere assertion strikes me as banal. But it would be erroneous to assume that only actionable knowledge is true knowledge, and that there is no knowledge worthy of the name that is not applied or, in principle, applicable.

According to this theory of knowledge, if the fix made possible through the application of knowledge is successful, it serves as a test for the validity of knowledge; if the fix fails, the knowledge leading to failure is not valid. In its extreme version, this means that one knows only what one can control through the application of material or behavioral technologies. This, surely, is the ultimate vulgarization of an idea.

Relevance, with a capital R, because its immanent subjectivism makes inter-subjective and, therefore, social knowledge impossible, breeds its own destruction. But the problems of converting knowledge into action would not go away if we were to just ignore them. These problems are serious and will have our attention in the future as they have had in the past. The same goes for the term "relevant" itself. We cannot simply expunge it from the lexicon. I would not call it a nonsense term. But precisely because "relevant" is a syntactical term, its location in the grammar of political discourse is a critical aspect of its proper use. It is in this connection that the term's vulgarization has been especially harmful.

In its most vulgar epistemological version, being relevant seems to mean something like this: determine what in the affairs of nature or society is Relevant, with a capital R, and proceed from there in building theories, doing research, and pursuing practical applications. Relevance, then, is something given, an axiom, that is good or virtuous and justifies what one is doing.

I want to argue just the opposite, namely that the determination of whether what one is doing is relevant does not and cannot precede one's thinking, research, or action—but follows it. One does not know whether one's work is or is not relevant until one has thought about and worked hard on a problem and tried to solve it. Just working on a problem, then, no matter how relevant it may appear to one because it cries out for solution, as so many of our social and environmental problems do, does not necessarily mean that one is being relevant.

One is relevant, of course, in the sense in which anything one does can be relevant that is not totally random behavior—seeing a movie, playing golf, reading a mystery, or just sitting in a rocking chair contemplating one's life. In this special sense, because everything one does is relevant, the term is trivial.

It is really not until the long-range consequences or side effects of one's activity are felt and subjected to critical evaluation that the relevance of the activity can be ascertained. We do not know in advance whether our teaching and research are relevant because we do not know what the effects of our teaching will be or what our research findings will be, how our teaching complements the teaching of others, or how our research findings will fit in with the findings of others. I come to the conclusion, therefore, that rather than being a cheap commodity on the market of syntactical terms, relevance is a most expensive commodity that one cannot appropriate without cost.

What I am arguing for, if argue I must, is that we restore the concept of relevance to the status of an objective or at the least intersubjective term in the syntax of social discourse. This means that we use the term once more contextually, for the syntax of social discourse is necessarily contextual. Let me suggest what I mean by the syntax of social discourse.

Every bit of current knowledge and every current human act is embedded in a historical context. There is, therefore, always the question of the *relevance of past events*. One could argue that historical reference is relevant only if it shows "how things have come to be what they are" rather than "how things have actually been."

Like most such dualisms, the dualism between antiquarian and relevant history is false. For how can one know how things have come to be what they are if one does not know what they have been? The fact that almost every generation of historians rewrites history, that history as a mode of approach to human affairs is intrinsically revisionist, answers my question.

Antiquarianism, though often used as a pejorative term, may have a relevance of its own that cannot be prejudged because new perspectives are likely to serve as transformers of the allegedly antiquarian into the allegedly relevant. In the perspective of time, propositions about the past cannot be arbitrarily defined as relevant or not relevant. It is in the nature of history that its constraints are flexible because they are subject to reinterpretation.

Second, every bit of current knowledge and every current act is embedded in the future. There is, therefore, the question of the *relevance of future events*. The overwhelming characteristic of the future is that it is not known. One might rightly ask, therefore, how something that is not known can be relevant or how one can be relevant to something that is not known. There seems to be a way out of this dilemma, and it involves, of course, the elaboration of mental constructs of the future.

These constructs may be apocalyptic visions, or they may be technological utopias, or they may be ideological images like the classless society, or they may be, like Lasswell's "developmental constructs," complex orientational maps constructed from trend-lines, scientific propositions and goal values. Whatever their mode of elaboration, constructs of the future have no truth value, but they can be used and are used as comprehensive frames of reference for orientation in the present.

But it would be a mistake to assume that only conduct that takes place or is investigated in the context of a future construct is relevant. To assume this would be to ignore, first, that not all future states can be envisaged; and second, that constructs of the future are at best hypotheses and, therefore, subject to falsification. It may well be, therefore, that what in the future perspective appears to be irrelevant may yet, when the future becomes actualized, turn out to be relevant; and what may appear relevant today may appear to be irrelevant tomorrow.

Finally, there is the question of the *relevance of the present* in knowledge and action. I come to the present last because here we face the most difficult and problematical test of relevance. Much as present events appear to us so direct, so self-evident, and so common-sensical as not to require empirical confirmation, the present is more open to error and bias than either past or future.

This is so, it seems to me, not only because we are involved in the present and must, of necessity, act in the present before the returns are in, but also because the present, unlike the past and the future, is only a very temporary and insignificant speck in the processes of change that link past and future. More than the past and the future, the present is exceptionally fugitive and perishable, and it is a veritable graveyard of false or falsified observations, conceptions, and propositions.

Much as acting and working in the present may give us a subjective sense of personal security, the present is in fact filled with insecurities. This is the reason, perhaps, why so much of what we say and do in the present is said and done with so much emotion and contention. Add to this the fact that how we see the present is invariably colored by our experiences of the past and our images of the future, and it becomes clear why the present is so elusive as a criterion of relevance.

In the syntax of social discourse then, "being relevant" as a property of knowledge and action is an emergent phenomenon rather than something immanent in knowledge and social action. Intervening between scientific knowledge and social action is invariably a long chain of intermediate steps that must be taken before knowledge can be translated into action. These intervening steps involve a technology that is subject to its own possibly autonomous laws of development.

If it is difficult to be precise, in the predictive sense, about the relevance of scientific knowledge to social problems, it is even more difficult to anticipate the relationship between social science and the social technology needed in the attack on social problems. In the field of law, for instance, who would want to be certain about the relationship between legal theory and such operative technologies as the administration of criminal justice or quasi-judicial regulation? I am not asking a rhetorical question. There is considerable evidence that mechanical and electrical engineering are possible without great reliance on the "relevant" scientific discoveries, and I think one could show this to be equally true of social, political, and legal "engineering." If this is so, and if you will now permit me to ask a rhetorical question, does this mean that social or legal theory and basic research are expendable because they may not immediately contribute to the solution of social problems?

Basic social theory and research, on the one hand, and social technologies, on the other hand, are different activities that are interrelated in complex and emergent ways whose outcome is never a foregone conclusion. Relevance, I argued earlier, follows rather than precedes the knowledge-making process; this is so, it now appears, because relevance is an emergent property of the configuration of events that may or may not link science and technology through time. The problem of relevance is not solved by a simplistic model to the effect that, somehow, social science leads to social technology which, on application, will solve our social problems. The model promises what it cannot deliver.

No "Credo of Relevance" or sloganeering about "Knowledge into Action" will be of much help. As long as the problem of knowledge is unsolved (and I think it is unsolved), as long as the problem of values is unsolved (and I think it is unsolved), and as long as the problem of the relationship between knowledge and values is unsolved (and I think it is unsolved), social science, like all knowledge-making disciplines, is ill-advised to give up its posture of dispassionate inquiry in favor of a politically expedient and socially opportune definition of knowledge, regardless of whether the pressure for such definition comes from an established elite, benevolently interested groups, self-appointed tribunes of the people, or the people itself.

7 SKILL REVOLUTION AND CONSULTATIVE COMMONWEALTH

My vision is a commonwealth in which human needs are discovered, human purposes formulated, and human problems handled by political processes better adapted to the requirements of a rapidly changing technological society[1] than are participative, representational, or bureaucratic processes alone. I am not saying that this commonwealth is one in which human needs are satisfied, human purposes achieved, and human problems solved. There is a world of difference between discovering and satisfying needs, between formulating and achieving purposes, between handling and solving problems. The vocabulary is experiential rather than existential, processual rather than programmatic.

My argument is that the "consultative commonwealth"[2] is at least one probable outcome of the relationship between the skill revolution of modern times and some of the socially problematic consequences of modern technology. The consultative commonwealth is not an inevitable outcome of contemporary trends. It is, however, a plausible construct—more optimistic than Lasswell's construct of the "garrison state,"[3] and more pessimistic than Bennis's construct of the "temporary society."[4] My task is to explore some of the logical and empirical linkages between the skill revolution, an empirical phenomenon, and the consultative commonwealth, a developmental conception of the future.[5]

SKILL REVOLUTION

The skill revolution of the last hundred years is one of the significant factors in the development of industrial and technological society. Many occupations, and especially the oldest and still most prestigious among them—the professions of law, of the clergy, of the academy, and medicine—have their roots in a distant past.[6] What is new, and what not even Emile Durkheim envisaged when he sought to explain the consequences of the division of labor for society,[7] is the incredible specialization in and proliferation of occupations that have accompanied industrial and technological developments. Harold Lasswell refers to this set of events as skill revolution and sees it as the basis for an observational standpoint in the study of politics "which cuts across the conventional categories of class and nation."[8]

The emphasis on skill is not to provide an alternative but a complementary frame of reference for the observation of social and political situations. An integrative view of society and politics cannot neglect nation and class as both significant social realities and analytic categories. But cutting across these realities and categories is skill specialization which, it is clear, does not stop at national boundaries or class barriers. It is as much a part of social change in the United States as in the Soviet Union,[9] and in the white-collar middle class as in the blue-collar working class.[10]

Skill specialization is probably the best directly available indicator of social and technological changes as behavioral dimensions. It has the virtue of empirical concreteness and relatively easy operational specification at the level of individual behavior. It therefore facilitates predictions about the future of political organization and processes in technological societies, regardless of their formal constitutional regimes.

Research on the political implications of the skill revolution has varying scholarly objectives. Lasswell was primarily interested in the rise and decline of skill elites for an explanation of the distribution of political values and the political transformation of societies.[11] Because scientific or other knowledge, higher education, and rational intelligence are important values, some analysts use similar notions to predict the emergence of societies in which owners, workers, or consumers have lost, and managers, scientists, or technologists have gained, control of the means of political power.[12] They do so by rather fanciful leaps of the imagination, not to mention neglect of intervening or contravening social processes. Changes in the composition of social and political elites will not be suspended in the future. But these changes rarely bring with them the one-tailed transformations that are so resolutely predicted.

The permeation of society's public and private spheres by the old professions and many new skill groups is likely to continue in the foreseeable future. Yet, it is premature to speak, as Frederick C. Mosher does, of "the professional state,"[13] at least in the sense that the professions will, in Daniel Bell's terms, constitute "the leadership of the new society."[14] It is a fragile presupposition that the possessors of new skills or specialized old skills will necessarily be dominant, if not exclusive, holders of political power. Tendencies contrary to the skill revolution evoked in response to social malfunctionings of technological society may attenuate or dissipate the concentration of power in the hands of those who have the new skills and specialized knowledge.

Imaginative extrapolations of trends in the structure and distribution of skills are conducive to the creation of benevolent or malevolent utopias; but constructs of the future are useful only to the extent that they permit us to orient ourselves meaningfully and correctly in the present. Apocalyptic visions of the future have just the opposite effect. They disorient the beholder and make it impossible for him to observe and explain the world as a prelude to predicting what it is likely to be or changing it in a preferred direction. What is needed to make research on the political implications of the skill revolution significant is a construct of the future that breaks with the familiar linear extrapolations of the effect of the skill revolution on the transformation and distribution of political power. The concept of the consultative commonwealth is such an alternative construct.

Research guided by the construct of the consultative commonwealth does not focus simply on the appearance of new elites whose influence is grounded in the possession of socially, economically, or politically useful skills and esoteric knowledge. Rather, it concentrates on the attitudes, orientations, and, especially, modes of conduct in their relationships with others that skill specialists bring to the task of governance. If skill specialists are asked to help in the manipulation of social problems and in the delivery of human services, not their positions in the hierarchies of power but their ways of doing things deserve our close research attention. This focus does not preclude other types of investigation into the political implications of the skill revolution. However, with a few exceptions, political scientists have not been much concerned with the political behavior of individual professionals,[15] or with professional associations as what Corinne L. Gilb calls "private governments,"[16] or with professional organizations as conventional pressure groups.[17] There is, then, a gap in our knowledge of the political implications of the skill revolution at the micro level of the individual as well as at the macro level of society.

Research on the professions promises to be a fascinating entry point into some problematic aspects of social structure and social change. The demographic and biographical approaches to the study of elites have not yielded the hoped-for results in contributing to an understanding of social and political change: The demographic approach is too aggregative and conceals more than it reveals at the level of the individual;[18] the biographical approach is too molecular and reveals more than is needed at the level of society.[19] Because politics is an emergent coefficient of the skill revolution, the professions are important topics of investigation;[20] for specializing professions are critical interstitial structures between the individual person and society.

If the emphasis is on those occupations conventionally called professions, it is not because there is a sharp dividing line between them and other vocations, or because the professions may in fact occupy positions of power and prestige in social and political systems.[21] It is because the consultative processes stemming from professionalization in the wake of the skill revolution and the modes of conduct normally associated with professionalism have crystallized more fully in the professions and paraprofessions.[22] The strenuous efforts made by many occupations to achieve professional status, whatever such status may mean to them, are further indications of the political implications of the continuing revolution in skills for the governance and servicing of modern societies.[23]

FUTURE-IN-COMING: EMERGENCIES

The consultative commonwealth is only a tentative construct, but among alternative models of the shape of political things to come it is more persuasive than most others. It is more persuasive because its emergence can be observed at the micro level of individual professional behavior. This is not to accept the convenient and comfortable assumption that present trends or countertrends will continue indefinitely into the future. Far from it. The weakness of futuristic extrapolation of trends is its neglect of the puzzling problem of how past, present, and future are connected in human action.[24]

Scenarios of the future are never played out as expected. There are two methodological points to be made about the construct of the consultative commonwealth. First, though a construct of the future, it is tutored by theory and empirical research. Its utility is to be judged not by its predictive power, for the future is not known and can therefore not be used to test derivative hypotheses. Rather, its utility must be judged by its ability to give rise to research and thought in the present that may be relevent to the future.

Second, not only is the future unknown but the laws of social development leading to the future are unknown. Every construct of the future, therefore, makes assumptions about the developmental process. The developmental model underlying the construct of the consultative commonwealth assumes oscillations between the polar ends of a temporal continuum. It assumes that there is no action without reaction, no force without resistance, no unity without plurality, no identity without difference, no growth without decay. The polar principle assumes that contradictory social processes are mutually entailed through time.[25]

The skill revolution and notably its vanguards, the professions, provide a suggestive point of departure. The professional is not a man who creates knowledge but a specialist who translates knowledge into action. The man of knowledge is a "longhair," and a longhair is by definition an impractical person. The professional is not a longhair, for he applies knowledge to practical concerns.[26] Unlike the man of knowledge, the professional "does something" that is oriented to the future in terms of goal values to be realized. The physician seeks to make the sick person healthy; the lawyer tries to recover a victimized person's rights; the professor as teacher strives to lead the student out of ignorance to understanding; the minister hopes to ease the penitent's road to salvation. This is not all that physicians, lawyers, professors, or ministers do, but their main task is to use their knowledge or experience in helping people meet problems which they cannot handle themselves;[27] and they do so by forming images of a desired future for their patients, clients, students, or parishioners.

Much of what the professional does is routine. It is routine because the problem at hand has usually been encountered before, or because the solution has been codified in a work of reference. But sometimes the professional confronts a genuinely new problem for which there is no ready-made solution. He then faces a situation of uncertainty that is, in effect, an emergent future because he must "do something" about it and cannot avoid the problem or postpone action.[28] In an emergency the professional will deal with the problem as best as he can, relying on his general skill, ingenuity, and what is called "intuition"—an estimate of the future. When the professional is involved in an emergency, the future is in the making. The future is simply the present-in-transition, and the present is the future-in-coming.

At the macro level of analysis, attention turns to the professions as collectivities and how they orient themselves to action in problematic social situations.[29] There is no lack of situations in contemporary society that call for professional intervention and the application of professional skills. How the professions relate themselves to problematic social and technological situations is, therefore, a matter of great significance for the future.

The relationship between the behavior of the professions as prototypical carriers of the skill revolution in a rapidly changing world and a viable construct of governing processes in the future is directly pertinent to many critical social problems—for instance, the formulation of public policies concerning and the adequate provision of those human services in fields like health, education, welfare, and safety that are the domain of the highly skilled occupations. These are not the only fields in which the skill revolution has consequences for the problems of society; but the provision of professional services, from medical care to legal aid, education, welfare, and protection—services on which modern society heavily depends for successful functioning—is inadequate in both distribution and quality.[30] Access to these services has come to be claimed as a common right of citizenship;[31] it is a right in conflict with differential privilege inherent in a segmented and stratified social structure. The realization of the right of access to professional services cannot be left, therefore, to the spontaneous working of the economic market.[32] Indeed, if there were no maldistribution and inadequacy in delivery, professional services in health, education, welfare, or protection would hardly be regarded as urgent matters of public concern.

The professions, paraprofessions, and subprofessions are sufficiently diverse, and their circumstances are sufficiently different, that it is dangerous to generalize about matters as complex and intricate as the provision of a multitude of services. This is why a developmental construct like the consultative commonwealth is useful, indeed necessary for research. For it should demonstrate that the problems involved in the provision of human services are not soluble simply by recourse to facile policy panaceas, faith in benign administrative palliatives, or dependence on political mobilization of inadequately served groups of clients.

This is not to say that these means are unimportant political change mechanisms or that their consequences, whichever, are unimportant. On the contrary, they are themselves issues in the relationship between skill revolution and consultative commonwealth.[33] For they are symptomatic of the strains and tensions between changing societal expectations concerning the delivery of human services, on the one hand, and difficulties facing the professionalization of these services, on the other hand.

POLARITY: PROFESSIONALIZATION AND DEPROFESSIONALIZATION

Skill revolution is not to be equated with professionalization; it does not in itself generate either the process of professionalization or the ideology of professionalism.[34] Because the most highly developed skills are in short supply, the skill structure will remain stratified; and those most highly placed in the skill structure, the professions, will be responsible for the delivery of human services and decision making concerning these services. The shape of the skill structure, however, will not remain the same.[35] Internal differentiation among those at the top of the skill hierarchy and the addition of new skill specialists are likely to broaden the structure and to increase the pool of trained personnel available for service, potentially enabling both the public and private sectors to respond more adequately to the novel problems created by high technology—either those that are foreseeable byproducts of scientifically grounded technology or those that are the unanticipated and socially harmful consequences of technological change.[36]

Although defining "profession" is important, it may become a passion, as it understandably is for those occupations that are striving for professional status.[37] In opting for a definition, one should let the problem at hand serve as the guide. The problem in this instance is to build a construct of the future commonwealth that pays attention not only to the professionalization of social or technical services and policy making, but also to a variety of counter-tendencies that are indicative of deprofessionalization.

On the one hand, the increasing application of scientific knowledge, technical skill, and rational intelligence will professionalize the delivery of human services and bring professionals into the policy-making process, in both the public and private sectors.[38] Moreover, if present trends continue, the provision of a great variety of services to all citizens will be high on the agenda of politics. The availability of a basic body of abstract knowledge with connected skills, and the performance of services, then, are the defining properties of what is meant by profession, and the patterns of behavior or conduct associated with these properties are the building blocks of the consultative commonwealth.[39] In this perspective, the internal transformation of the older professions and the appearance of some new professions, responding to changes in scientific or technical knowledge and the demand for new services, are significant social and political processes.

On the other hand, professional skill and expertise are being challenged in these fields by counter-currents to professional approaches released in the name of consumerism, community power, and open access for previously excluded groups, especially women and ethnic minorities.[40] First, because professionalism is a *political* ideology, it motivates not only those who use it to protect their social status and those who aspire to higher social status, but also those who see in professionalism a defense of the *status quo*.[41] And second, professionalization—the transformation of an occupation into a profession—is a *political* process because it involves, among other things, a quest for statutory legitimacy and related publicly-sanctioned privileges as well as for public acceptance. It is therefore always exposed to the vagaries of politics.

Ironically, both professionalizing and deprofessionalizing tendencies derive from two major changes in the classical relationship between professional and client. First, professionals increasingly work in and for organizations with clients who are not their employers but rather the consumers of their services. And second, professional dominance in the professional's relationship with clients is contained by the appearance of client organizations which presume to speak for individual or collective clients.

A number of derivative consequences follow: As professionals come to work in political milieux, politicization of the professional-client relationship tends to undermine professional autonomy. The challenges encountered from clientele organizations, with their own ideas about the provision of services and performance, tend to undercut professional authority. The need of professionals to protect their own interests may lead to unionization, which, in the view of some, endangers the professional norm of commitment to the public interest. The location of professionals in bureaucratic organizations with their tendency to inertia and ritualistic behavior can easily thwart experimentation, innovation, and discretion.[42] Finally, the built-in obsolescence of professional skills in a rapidly changing scientific and technological culture makes for tensions within and between the professions that weaken professional credibility and legitimacy.

At the same time, society will also be much more demanding in its expectations concerning the delivery of services. The demand for more and better services combined with tendencies toward the deprofessionalization of services, represents a paradox. Rather than improving service, deprofessionalization would have just the opposite effect. This is so because it would involve an altogether irrational reversal of normal expectations. The normal chain follows a sequence in which a client in need of help seeks out a competent specialist whose professional authority he accepts and to whom he grants decisional autonomy. Deprofessionalization reverses this chain, because its main effect is to reduce professional autonomy. But reduced autonomy weakens professional authority; weakened authority devalues professional competence; and devalued professional skill will impoverish the quality of the service that is rendered.

In the perspective of contemporary counter-tendencies to professionalization, then, the consultative commonwealth would seem to breed the seeds of its own destruction and negate the promises of the skill revolution. Before accepting this dismal prospect, however, some other considerations are in order. One need not be a dialectician to recognize that deprofessionalizing tendencies in turn generate their own countervailing forces. The professions do not passively accept deprofessionalizing challenges, be they internal to a profession or external. They develop adaptive techniques and coping strategies that blunt the impact of deprofessionalization and, in fact, strengthen a profession's authority and autonomy.

The consultative commonwealth, in taking account of deprofessionalizing pressures in its consultative arrangements, also contains within itself the seeds of renewal.[43] It differs, then, from those constructs of the future society that are based on one sided extrapolations of either tendencies alone, or counter-tendencies alone, in the formation and circulation of skill elites. These models are deficient in two respects. First, they fail to recognize the dynamics of the polarity principle in the development of societies, especially those in the stage of advanced technology. And second, they neglect the normative capabilities of politics. However, even if deprofessionalizing tendencies are accounted for, it is more probable than not that the future commonwealth will be highly dependent on professional services.

Because increasing demand for services will continue to exceed available supply, the power of skill specialists is always balanced by new demands coming from dissatisfied clienteles. If all of this were only a matter of supply and demand in the economic sense, political science would not have much of a contribution to make to its understanding. But the problem of professional services is not just an economic question; it is also an eminently political question, for it involves relationships of authority and autonomy between those who provide and those who demand the services.

To appreciate the political issue, I take a clue from an insightful passage by that wise student of the occupations, Everett C. Hughes. Investigation of the challenges facing the professions and of their responses, Hughes suggested, "is study of politics in the very fundamental sense of studying constitutions. For constitutions are the fundamental relations between the effective estates which make up the body politic."[44] Professionals are involved in four constitutional relationships—with clients, with organizations, with their own colleagues, and with the larger society. The structures and functions of these relationships and the norms of professional conduct in a particular relationship, for the professional and his significant others, create political issues that differ a good deal from profession to profession, from one institutional setting to another, and from one set of relationships to the next. They should, therefore, be expected to have different consequences as one projects the consultative commonwealth of the future.

RELATIONSHIP WITH CLIENTS

Of all the professional's relationships, that with clients is of fundamental constitutional importance for the evolution of social institutions and public policies. The classical relationship between professional practitioner and client is contractual and in the nature of an exchange. The client takes the initiative in seeking out the professional and, by paying a fee, employs him to perform the desired service. Professions differ in their responses to client initiatives; but, in general, the relationship is assumed to be reciprocal.

As the interaction proceeds, however, the relationship is transformed. Once having "placed himself in the hands" of the professional, the client becomes a dependent. The client is still free to reject the professional's advice and help, but he does so at his own risk and, for all practical purposes, does not do it. Client behavior is important, then, in defining the professional's role. As long as the relationship is built on trust which, in turn, derives from the client's recognition of his own ignorance and the professional's competence, the client is willing to accept the practitioner's decisions concerning his needs. In effect, then, what was initially a functional relationship is transformed into an intrinsically hierarchical relationship. This transformation is overlooked by those who take a benign view of professional expertise as purely functional and who expect the infusion of expertise into the creation and delivery of human services to have *ipso facto* salubrious consequences for society.[45]

Because the relationship between professional and client is one of authority, in a generally democratic culture it is likely to be ambivalent, if not conflictual. Although, in essence, the client surrenders himself to the professional, neither party is fully comfortable. If the resulting ambivalence or conflict remains contained and does not seriously interfere with the service, it is because there also remains, in an open market, the possibility for the client to terminate the consultation or for the professional to withdraw his service. But if the market is restricted or state-controlled, and if free choice of services is impossible, tension and even hostility will characterize the professional-client relationship. Although maldistribution or substantive inadequacy of medical, legal, welfare, or protective services is the manifest target of current discontent, some of the dissatisfaction, especially among those who depend on state-provided and state-controlled services, stems from the tension built into the authority relationship.

Ambivalence and conflict may also arise because the client's perspective of professional service and what is brought to that perspective may differ from the professional's perspective in the first place. Because of this difference, as Hughes has noted, professionals, although "convinced that they themselves are the best judges, not merely of their own competence but also of what is best for the people for whom they perform services, are required in some measure to yield judgment of what is wanted to these amateurs who receive the services."[46]

Professionals are understandably reluctant to do this. If, therefore, the professional wishes to insist on the correctness of his own judgment, it is incumbent on him to mold client expectations of what constitutes proper service. More often than not, however, in order to make clients accept their authority, professionals rely for persuasion on institutional means, notably the doctrine of "free choice,"[47] rather than on professional ways.

Reliance on the authority of status exacerbates the professional-client relationship in the contemporary, democratizing environment. In the classical model, the environment in which professional-client interaction was played out did not consciously enter the relationship because professional and client could be assumed to share the same environment. Professionals, of middle-class status by definition, either served those above them in the class structure or those on their own level; and if they served the lower classes, their institutional authority was not questioned. Because of social class barriers, professionals found it difficult to empathize with the lower orders of society, even if they served them occasionally in charitable ways. It was the great genius of the Roman Catholic Church that by replicating in its own hierarchy the class structure of society, and by recruiting its servants from among all social classes to serve all social classes, it did not lose contact with its lower-class clienteles, even as democratization of the hierarchy provided for mobility within the ranks of the clergy.[48] Such rootedness in the total environment was never the case with physicians, lawyers, or professors, even after the social recruitment base was widened, precisely because institutional professionalization caused these professionals to consider themselves, and to be considered, middle-class in status. Identification with the middle class alienated professionals from the lower-class environment.

As a result of the extension of professional services to the working and lower classes, professionals now encounter clients whose perspective is very different from their own. The shock of recognizing the difference in environments is more or less shared in the different professions, and it has led to the belief that in at least some cases and situations not the individual client but his entire social environment requires professional treatment. Credit for discovering the salience of the environment in professional practice must be given to social work, but the discovery has now considerable influence in law, medicine, and university teaching. In the academy, retreating into the "ivory tower" is no longer an appropriate professional posture as it is recognized that an environment favorable to the pursuit of knowledge cannot be taken for granted.

The discovery of the environment and the movement toward professional intervention in the environment has created a profound crisis in the professions. If the environment must be changed before the client's problems can be treated, the role of the client in the relationship with the professional comes to be redefined. This is so because clients are themselves a part of the environment and, as a result, are seen as important components in shaping the environment. The client perspective intrudes into the professional-client relationship more than it ever has. Much of the current crisis in professional services turns on the nature of client participation in decisions concerning these services. The professional schools, sensitive to this, increasingly try to give instruction not only in subjects that relate to the environment in which the prospective professional will work, but also in subjects that provide him with skills in organization, negotiation, human relations, and so on.[49]

If the professionals fail to persuade clients of what constitutes proper service, they leave themselves open to client demands of what proper service should be. They allow themselves to be pressured into conformity with client expectations, even if it violates professional criteria of service. As Hughes noted, this is especially likely in periods of social unrest: "In time of crisis, there may arise a general demand for more complete conformity to lay modes of thought, discourse, and action."[50]

The pressure for conformity to lay perspectives comes from people who occupy higher- or lower-status positions in society than does the professional himself. The legal profession, itself highly stratified, is especially exposed to client perspectives.[51] In the academy some professors yield to student pressures for conformity to their interpretations of what learning and knowledge are all about by lowering standards and "being with it," sometimes assuming student styles and demeanor. Deprofessionalization has become a burning issue in social work. As one critic writes,

> the new activist spirit in social work downgrades professional practice, which is ineffective in dealing with social problems. In place of professionalism the activists offer the idea that revolution will create change more rapidly than social work practice, which may be correct. But this is not what the profession prepares one to do, nor should it.[52]

Professional consultants at the highest levels of policy-making often conform to policymakers' wishes and predilections, permitting their knowledge to be used for societal objectives that from a professional perspective may be undesirable.[53]

Perhaps the problem of differing perspectives between professional and client is insoluble. If so, there will always be an element of conflict in the relationship. If the professional only relies on his authority without further efforts at persuasion, the client is in no position to evaluate the grounds of the professional's advice. Under these conditions, professionals will jealously guard their monopoly on expert knowledge and status, but clients will not comply with professional advice and, in some cases, they will revolt against the prescriptions of the experts. Most recently there has been a trend toward reducing professional autonomy and enabling clients to enforce professional responsibility in the provision of services that has hitherto been the professions' own prerogative. Professionals, in turn, resent lay interference, especially when, as in teaching or librarianship, clients can bring pressure on policy-making, elected boards. In this context, present trends toward unionization of professionals takes on an aspect that goes beyond the bread-and-butter unionism of old, for it is as much a matter of politics as of economics. If professionals feel that laymen make undue demands in areas of competence they consider their own, the collective withdrawal of services—traditionally frowned upon as "unprofessional conduct"—is a very real possibility.[54]

All of these developments could have possibly disastrous consequences for professional service. If the client cannot distinguish between the professional's authority that is based on expertise and his authority that is based on status or power, the basic trust on which the professional-client relationship is founded becomes eroded. In revolting against the professional's status and power, however, the client also revolts, if inadvertently, against professional knowledge and competence.

RELATIONSHIP WITH ORGANIZATIONS

The professional increasingly encounters the client not in private but in organizational settings.[55] The original professions—clergy, law, academy, and medicine—had been characterized as *freie Berufe* or "free callings." Freedom referred to independence from organizational constraints. Although clergymen and academics depended for support on church and university, the professions were assumed to be free in two senses: first, the professional's behavior was guided by norms created by himself and designed to protect him against external pressures—the professions enjoyed autonomy; and second, the professional worked alone with individuals by applying his best professional judgment and was unencumbered by responsibility to an employing organization—the professions had authority.

The professional's work today is likely to take place in organizational and institutional settings that restrict his freedom more than was the case before the skill revolution reached its apogee.[56] The professional in these settings is subject to two modes of authority—organizational-hierarchical authority in the hands of administrative officials, and the authority of skill and competence exercised by professional colleagues, both inside and outside the organization.[57] The two forms of authority are conflictual and make for stress and strain in professional conduct vis-à-vis administrators, colleagues, and clients.[58] As a result, "disjunctive processes" are widespread.[59] Speaking of the academy, for instance, Logan Wilson notes:

> Even though academicians are professional men and women enjoying a high degree of independence as specialists per se, they function within an institutional framework which evaluates, ranks, and rewards them in terms of their presumed value to the organization. The whole process is so complex that it is inevitably a

source of misunderstanding, and the results are unavoidably a further source of real or alleged grievance to some individuals.[60]

If this is true in the highly permissive context of the university, it is surely even truer in the highly organized contexts of public or private bureaucracies.

If the professional's identification and commitment are stronger than his organizational loyalty,[61] rather than being threatened by bureaucracy, it may be professionalism that disturbs administrative ways of doing things. Hierarchical authority in administrative decision making is being undermined, Francis E. Rourke suggests, by "the growing power of skilled professions in the work of public bureaucracy. . . . Professionalism is rapidly succeeding politics as the principal source of decentralization of authority in American bureaucracy. A subordinate who is master of esoteric skills is no easier to dominate than one backed by a strongly entrenched group of political supporters."[62]

This transformation is by no means self-evident, because the problem of coordinating specialized expertise in organizations was long obscured by the ready availability of what Max Weber called "legal-rational authority" or bureaucracy.[63] The most obvious answer to the question of how best to coordinate specializations leads to the bureaucratic model that stresses rationalization, routinization, and standardization. Despite wide variations in practice, the organizational settings in which professionals work—hospitals, law firms, government bureaus, research laboratories, corporation offices, labor unions, religious organizations, universities, engineering firms, and so on—remain basically bureaucratic. What is happening, however, is an interpenetration of bureaucratization and professionalization—"the culture of bureaucracy invades the professions; the culture of professionalism invades organizations."[64]

In the broadest historical perspective, skill revolution, professionalization, and bureaucracy are symptoms of the same secular trend in Western society which Talcott Parsons describes as making for rationality, impersonality, functional specificity, and universalism.[65]

If bureaucratic means of coordination had not been as well developed as they were when the skill revolution reached the professions, consultative modes of coordination as immanent properties of professionality might have emerged sooner than they did. However, bureaucratization and professionalization are possibly isomorphic in structure and characterized by convergent tendencies with respect to authority—"professional authority is more similar to bureaucratic authority than is generally recognized. . . ."[66] While it is difficult empirically to disentangle the two phenomena because of their interdetermination,[67] the isomorphism between bureaucratic and professional authority, if true, casts doubt on some romantic notions that organization theorists have about the superiority of functional over hierarchical forms of coordination. If only professional or functional criteria were dominant in organization, bureaucratic pathologies like arbitrariness, unimaginativeness, authoritarianism, rigidity, and so forth, would miraculously yield to creativity, flexibility, involvement, and so on.[68] That the professions themselves may be tainted by bureaucratic tendencies is, therefore, a sobering thought.

In addition, the organizational context of professional practice is a source of deprofessionalizing tendencies that are as yet little understood. Deprofessionalization, in this connection, means loss of professional identity. There are two contradictory possibilities. On the one hand, loss of professional identity may be due to initial overidentification with and subsequent overreaction against the organization. This makes it difficult to separate out the alleged evils of bureaucracy from the alleged evils of professionalism. Attacks within the professions on "professionalism" which is sometimes seen, probably rightly, as a conservative force, are easily misplaced. At least it is not at all clear whether they are directed at the bureaucratic or at the professional component of the organization that is seen as requiring change if policy formulation and human services are to be improved.

Deprofessionalization in this sense has become a very real issue, though it varies a good deal from profession to profession, depending to a large degree on a profession's involvement in public policy as a condition for the realization of its professional goals. For instance, a profession like social work, which is directly affected by public policy, has a strong stake in welfare policies and public financial support. Attacks on professionalism have become an almost endemic feature of discourse in social work. In teaching at the primary and secondary levels, the long quest for professional status seems to have abated in recent years as teachers turn to unionization rather than professionalization as a means to improve their working conditions, raise their social status, and influence public policy.[69] By contrast, however, technical professionals are reported to evince "a complete lack of consensus on what needs to be done," with unionizers in one camp and "professional purists" in the other.[70]

On the other hand, loss of professional identity may be due to an inability to discover a specific client in organizational settings. A person's sense of identity is in no small part determined for him by the significant others with whom he interacts. Loss of professional identity is inevitable if the professional cannot identify the clients whom he is supposed to serve.

In the classical model of the profession, the professional was expected to serve a particular client, usually in a face-to-face encounter, and by serving the client to serve, in a vague way, society. As long as client interests and societal interests could be assumed to be the same, there seemed to be no problem. Again, this consonance varied from profession to profession. Physicians, for instance, had little trouble in this respect, at least until recently. Health was a value on which a social consensus existed, and in treating his patient, the physician was serving society. Today the conflict over abortion and the disagreement about the artificial prolongation of life have created considerable affective dissonance about the value of life. Similarly, while justice is presumably the consensual aim of the legal profession, it has long been recognized that what may be good for the lawyer's client may not advance the best interests of society.

The complexity of modern social and technological problems defies the simplicity of the traditional model. "Client uncertainty" is so pervasive that it not only makes for deprofessionalization but prevents some aspiring occupations from becoming professionalized. Who, for instance, is the client of the corporate manager who so desperately seeks professional status? Is it the employing corporation, the stockholders, the consumers, or society at large?[71] University professors are highly sensitive to client uncertainty. Who are their clients? The students whom they teach, the colleagues who benefit from their research, the governing board who pays their salaries, the publishers for whom they write texts, the government agency or business with whom they consult, or society at large? Client uncertainty obscures what providing a service means, and it suggests the great potential for conflict in the provision of services.

In some circumstances, the professional serving various clients is under enormous pressure to help some but not other clients. University professors have been subjected to much pressure, if not force, to refuse service to some clients whose policies or goals other clients disapprove.[72] This type of pressure for *selective* service undermines professional autonomy, and without autonomy—the right to decide whom to serve—the very concept of profession is meaningless.

RELATIONSHIP WITH COLLEAGUES

The professional's best defense against client uncertainty caused by organizational complexity is his identification with colleagues. Strong collegial ties are an important requisite of professional autonomy. Yet the professional's relationship with colleagues is by no means always simple. It is *relatively* simple if two professional colleagues enter a reciprocally advantageous consultative relationship, for it is mutually deferential and consensual in the sense that both partners share a common perspective. As a result, control problems like those arising in the professional-client relationship because of the confusion between the authority of expertise and the authority of status do not occur. The ideally limiting case seems to be the kind of relationship that exists when one scientist consults another. Indeed, Hughes and Parsons suggest that there is a basic structural difference between science and profession which makes for differing authority relationships between scientific colleagues, on the one hand, and professional colleagues, on the other.[73] It seems preferable to make this role differentiation less sharp. The university-based scholar in his role as teacher stands in a professional relationship to his colleagues because they share a student clientele; the practicing attorney sometimes stands in a scholarly relationship to his colleagues at the bar or on the bench.

Nevertheless, as an analytic distinction, the differentiation between the scholar-scientist and the professional with clients is suggestive; it calls attention to different control mechanisms and consultative relationships. Scientists control each other directly and publicly. They do so by frank and open reporting of the assumptions that go into the gathering of evidence, of the methods used in analyzing the evidence, and of the evidence itself.[74] Scientific associations are primarily learned societies whose principal goals are to publish journals and hold meetings in order to facilitate scientific communication and exchange.[75] Although there are standards as to what is good or bad scientific work, there is no such thing as a code of ethics for scientists in their role as scientists. Of course, when scientists become policy advisers or perform services for public or private organizations, they take on the professional role and come to be concerned about "proper professional conduct."

In contrast to pure scientific knowledge, much professional knowledge is a kind of tacit know-how that cannot be readily communicated and evaluated and that may even be secret or confidential.[76] Only extraordinary cases of abuse in professional behavior generally come within the purview of collegial control. Because direct control as in relationships among scientists is not available, the professions seek to maintain professional standards through their organizations, codes of ethics, and government-sanctioned licensing. Yet the professional control mechanisms are weak. Although holding a professional license implies professional authenticity, codes of ethics are poorly enforced,[77] and membership in professional associations, being voluntary, is far from universal.[78]

A profession as a whole, then, is by no means a community of like-minded equals or an *imperium in imperio* as is sometimes claimed. It is a complex aggregate of skill specialists working in a great variety of settings and differentiated not only in function but also in esteem, status, authority, and influence.[79] Specialization and subspecialization in the wake of the skill revolution accentuate these tendencies.

Stratification within and between the professions, as in all status systems, restricts vertical communication. As a result, although interprofessional collaboration may be needed—as in the modern hospital where physicians depend on nurses, technicians, pharmacists, and other specialists—professionals of higher status may not get the cooperation they need from lower-status professionals.[80] Stratification reduces society's potential for consultation even if there is growing professionalization of human services.

Whether efforts to democratize the professions will improve the delivery of services is an open question. It is probably true, as Cynthia F. Epstein observes in discussing the entry of women into the professions, that

> many of today's gifted young professionals are no longer eager to enter the traditional inner corps of the professions. . . . This seems to be particularly so in law and medicine, where there are signs of a breakdown in the collegial structure and

an increasing challenge to the traditional insistence on recruits of particular types.[81]

But this may actually reinforce already existing oligarchical tendencies in the professions. If the professional associations are to be the guardians of professional standards and interests, those best qualified in terms of professional rather than extraneous criteria will continue to emerge as professional leaders. This will mean, as Roberto Michels would predict, that associational oligarchs will continue to rule, though their ideological blinders may be different from those worn by their predecessors. If the leadership of the professions is to constitute an influential elite of merit, however, it will emerge not from the application of plebiscitary techniques to professional control but from consultative understandings and arrangements. As Wilbert E. Moore has put it well, "the criteria in organizational advancement tend to be mixed, and, as in all representational systems, the very attributes that distinguish a man from his colleagues may set him apart from their interests, rather than representing them with exceptional skills."[82]

RELATIONSHIP WITH SOCIETY

Society's dependence on specialized and skilled professional services is balanced, in a constitutional sense, by the professions' dependence on society for accreditation. Accreditation, a profession's success in having "license" to perform its services, is contingent on society's satisfaction with professional performance. Involved is not just the legal permission to practice a trade, with its complementary prohibition to others who do not have the requisite skills; also involved is the profession's legitimacy to carry out a "mandate" for society. This means that only the profession, and no one else, can collectively presume "to tell society what is good and right for the individual and for society at large in some aspect of life."[83]

The relationship between profession and society is in a deepening crisis. At issue is the profession's authority within its area of competence. Authority is a precondition for the exercise of the profession's mandate to determine what is in the best interests of society as a kind of collective client. At issue also is the profession's autonomy from societal constraints which, in this connection, means that professional performance can only be judged by the profession itself, for only the profession is qualified to do so.[84] Professional authority and autonomy are threatened by a number of developments over which a profession has little control. One development, it was noted, is the organizational context in which professionals work, and in which the profession's functional and the organization's hierarchical authority come into conflict. Another development is a generally more competitive environment. An old profession may encounter competition from new professions or semi-professions whose work is adjacent or overlapping. In the case of the legal profession, for instance, "tax accountants, trust officers in banks, insurance adjusters, marital counselors, labor arbitrators, and a host of others are engaged in matters that are in part legal."[85] What is challenged is the profession's claim to exclusive mastery of a body of unique knowledge and related skills.

Finally, professional services come to be seen not as purchasable private goods but as public goods with accessibility to all as a matter of right. Clients have come to the realization that professionals not only do things *for* them but also *to* them.[86] This varies of course considerably from client to client. While the big Wall Street law firm can do little to its corporate client but give it bad advice, the social-welfare worker has almost absolute control over the poor welfare mother on relief.[87] While the corporation has effective sanctions over the law firm, the solitary welfare recipient has practically none. Like corporate clients, organizations of individual clients (e.g., welfare rights organizations) have come to demand a voice in the professional decisions affecting them.

This demand jeopardizes one of the professions' most cherished prerogatives—the authority to determine client needs. To protect this prerogative, the professions have always sought to justify themselves in terms of the mandate given them by society. Indeed, the mandate of service in the public interest more than authoritative expertise has been the justification for insisting on autonomy. Yet a profession's mandate is always probationary, in very much the same sense in which an elected representative's term of office is probationary.

A profession's persistence as a "community within a community" is contingent, as any mandate is contingent, on continued ability to satisfy the public trust placed in it as the custodian of esoteric competences.[88] At least until recently, the professions were given this public trust. The legal profession was expected to be directly concerned with the administration of justice and relevant legislation; and the medical profession was expected to concern itself with the organization, distribution, and remuneration of medical services.

Their public roles expose the professions to public criticism, and their public mandate has come to be questioned. The professions are accused of not meeting societal expectations of proper policy or service, and their role as agents of the public interest in particular areas of policy or service is being attacked on the ground that they have been more self-serving than other-serving.[89] This criticism, Parsons suggests, tends to confuse private motivation with the institutional setting that differentiates professionals from those who, like businessmen, pursue private gain.[90] But the professions organize themselves as interest-group associations in the same way as do labor unions or business organizations. And although one should not confuse a profession as such with its associational instruments, the professions have been no less "selfish," whatever this means, than other interest groups.[91] Public sensitivity to the professions' political involvement in favor of their own rather than public interests is widespread.

That they are in trouble as trustees of the public interest has not gone unnoticed in the professions themselves. How to respond to societal distrust of their integrity proves to be perplexing. Investigations conducted at Stanford over the last few years concerning the political behavior and attitudes of professionals in particular institutional settings or with respect to particular public issues, indicate much political ambivalence within the professions themselves.[92] In the ministry a "new breed" of activist clergymen feel that the churches should give forceful leadership on public issues.[93] City planners have come to realize that they "must be able to persuade, bargain, and compromise, lest decision makers listen to those who are better able to persuade, bargain, and compromise."[94] Law students evidently continue to prefer careers in the private sector to careers in the public sector, but extracurricular experience may be an increasingly important factor in determining their choice.[95] Counter groups in law and medicine organize law communes and people's clinics that challenge the traditional priorities of these professions.[96] Policy-oriented scientists "go public" and expand the scope of conflict over issues of public policy.[97] Journalists seem to be quite sensitive to the problem of how their reporting the news affects the success or failure of protest groups in different fields of welfare.[98] Black professionals are concerned about the effect of their work environment, whether predominantly black or white, on their leadership potential in home communities.[99] All of these studies reveal tensions that arise out of the relationship between the professions' presumed obligations to the public trust and the increasing criticism of their work both inside and outside the professions.

The Stanford studies show that ritualistic invocation of the professions' mandate to serve the public interest is not sufficient to help them out of their quandary. For it is the definition of the public interest that *is* the quandary. The problem of definition is of course not unique to the professions.[100] In the absence of an accepted formal definition, contextual treatment seems most appropriate.

The context in which most professionals worked was long pervaded, and to a large extent still is pervaded, by the ethos of social and economic individualism. This ethos set limits to the services which professionals sought to render and were expected to render. In effect, service in the public interest was defined in terms of those who could afford professional services. This meant that the professions largely served the interests of the affluent society rather than the interests of what Michael Harrington has called "the other America."[101] The professions were satisfied that they were serving the public interest if their services met "effective demand," that is, the demand of those who could purchase their services.

The definition of professional service in the public interest is changing, from an essentially economic to a social-moral content. The new definition refers to "unmet needs" rather than to effective demand. It is an open question whether the new definition will help the professions overcome the crisis in their relationship with society. On the one hand, if the professions succeed, by their own practices and the policies they are able to influence, in broadening the range and improving the quality of the services they provide for society, their claim to autonomy is strengthened rather than weakened. This is perhaps something that the American Bar Association and the American Medical Association have yet to learn.

On the other hand, the notion of unmet needs is sufficiently ambiguous to create new troubles. The substitution of unmet needs for effective demand gives the impression that one is somehow dealing with a self-evident, readily usable standard for judging professional performance. In fact, just the opposite is the case. Effective demand is an economic market phenomenon that, within its defined parameters, can be measured; unmet need is a moral criterion that is by no means easy to operationalize. In general, unmet needs become visible only when those whose needs are not met rise to the occasion, as happened in the sixties. Insofar, however, as the professions accept unmet needs as a criterion by which to judge the adequacy of human services, they also seem to admit that clients have a right to participate in the making of policies that had previously been their own professional mandate.[102]

PROTEST AND RESPONSE

In fact, what clients articulate are not unmet needs, but unmet wants. Client participation in decisions appropriately within the province of the professions violates the constitutional basis of the professional-client relationship. This basis cannot be democratic if professional service is to have any meaning. As T. H. Marshall has pointed out, "authority passes to the professional, who must give [the client] what he needs, rather than what he wants. The client, unlike the customer, is not always right."[103] If the protest movement of recent years is not to be a mere "revolution for the hell of it," its influence on the delivery of human services depends, as Michael Lipsky has persuasively shown, on increasing the bargaining ability of powerless groups in the arena of politics by building viable organizations and harnessing stable political resources. Protest as such is symptomatic of unmet needs, but it can only articulate demands.[104] It, therefore, does not absolve the professions from their responsibility to determine needs. Whatever other functions are served by protest, demands for community control and client participation in *professional* decision making are probably more a distraction than a remedy.[105] Community power as a panacea for solving the problems of professional service is at best ironic, for local sovereignty—whether in the name of the feudal prince or the common people—has always been a shibboleth of conservatism and reaction. As Wilbert Moore remarks, "decentralization does not end oligarchy; it only dissipates and therefore in a sense extends it."[106]

In the perspective of professionalism, the protest movement attacks something endemic in professional service. Hughes has pointed out that "in many occupations, the workers or practitioners (to use both a lower and a higher status term) deal routinely with what are emergencies to the people who receive their services."[107] If this is true of normal situations, it is even truer when service must be rendered to mass publics under bureaucratic conditions in times of crisis. The client's feeling of being neglected is not something easily dealt with. Although consultative forms of interaction between spokesmen for professional services and organized clienteles may be conducive to mutual understanding of this dilemma, it would be utopian under modern organizational conditions to expect an easy solution of the routine-versus-emergency problem.

Very much the same can be said of another problem to which Hughes has called attention—the problem of mistakes and failure. Sensitivity to the possibility of mistakes and failure is common to both the social worker in a local welfare agency and the economist on the President's Council of Economic Advisers. Mistakes harm both the professional and his client; the absence of clearcut criteria of success or failure makes the problem all the more perplexing. Clients tend to confuse the successful conclusion of the service with good professional work. For this reason professionals insist on peer judgment of their performance. The medical quack, the shyster lawyer, and the grandstanding professor will please their customers but not their colleagues. To protect themselves against mistakes, the professions place great emphasis on routine, ritual, etiquette, and approved ways of doing things. Referral to and consultation among colleagues serve the same function of minimizing risk. In this connection, the division of labor is not just technical but also psychological.

The volatility and sometimes violence of what has been called "the revolt of the client" are for some professionals traumatic experiences. Their consequences are difficult to foresee because it is impossible to separate out long-term secular changes in the professions from changes in response to immediate social pressures. For a time it appeared that the protest movement, as two sociologists concluded in 1969, "attacks the basic legitimacy of the occupational and institutional claims to power of the professional," on a number of grounds: "1) the expertise of the practitioners is inadequate, 2) their claims to altruism are unfounded, 3) the organizational delivery system supporting their authority is defective and insufficient, and 4) this system is too efficient and exceeds the appropriate bounds of its power."[108] Although this funeral oration was probably premature, the paradox of the last two points calls attention to at least one important problematic aspect of the skill revolution's impact on the provision of professional services in modern technological society.

Self-criticism within the professions has long been directed toward the growing fragmentation of services due to specialization and subspecialization.[109] The fragmentation of service is seen as a source of client discontent because it seems to depersonalize and standardize the professional-client relationship, making the client feel that he is merely an assembly of parts rather than a whole person with interrelated problems requiring an integrative solution. At least some professionals have therefore called for holistic treatment of the client that would restore his dignity as a whole person.[110]

Precisely the opposite argument has also been made. The protest movement is seen as opposed to restoring the client as a whole person through institutional co-ordinating mechanisms. "The client seems to be rejecting what he considers institutionalized meddling under the cover of professional concern," write Haug and Sussman; and they continue:

> Outreach programs from the client perspective have become out-grab. Students want to organize their own courses and call in the professional as a consultant. The "whole man" approach in medicine infringes on areas of social relations where clients consider themselves competent; patients want to turn to the doctor when in trouble, but not be bothered otherwise. This suggests that the client is demanding the right to define the problem, and then call upon the professional only as a specialist in a narrow domain.[111]

Though their evidence is flimsy, Haug and Sussman present a rather ingenious theory about the consequences of the client revolt as they describe it:

> . . . since the major thrust of the client revolt has been against the institutional concomitants of professionalism, including the tendency of the professional to extend his authority beyond the limits of his legitimated special expertise, one might predict a narrowing of professional authority to the most limited and eso-teric elements of his knowledge base. This is unlikely to mean, despite client-revolt rhetoric, that the professional will fully lose the core of his autonomy, the right to define the nature of the client's problem.Even if the client exercised his right to pick and choose the time and place of his use of the professional's exper-tise, once the client enters the interaction, the expert's knowledge of cause-effect will permit him to diagnose and respecify the original complaint or need into his terms.[112]

These analysts conclude, therefore, that the tension between professional and society can lead to deprofessionalization, but that "what the client demands— the professional as a limited consultant—may be less a curse than a blessing in disguise."[113]

There is something comforting in this theory. On th one hand, it does not contradict the skill revolution hypothesis of progressive specialization; on the other hand, it anticipates changes in the professional-client relationship which, on close inspection, seem to be radical without really being so. The theory may well be true.

Despite antiprofessional tendencies in the protest movement, a new balance in organized professional-client relations seems to be emerging. On the one hand, the protest movement comes to realize that it needs professional assistance. As Lipsky points out,

> the need for skilled professionals is not restricted to lawyers. . . . Protest groups may need architects and city planners to present a viable alternative to urban renewal proposals. They may need consultant assistance to present testimony concerning the inadequacy of governmental programs. They may need grantsmen to compete for federal and private philanthropic funds. . . .[114]

On the other hand, new developments within the professions in response to changing social values appear as reassertions of professional authority. Representation of client interests and their satisfaction through new professional roles rather than through direct client participation is the most noteworthy of these developments.[115]

The new "advocacy role" is available at both the level of individual service and societal policy making. In this role, the professional does not just respond to client demands and, by responding, serve society; rather, his task is to anticipate needs, initiate services, and improve society.

There are some real difficulties with the advocacy role. In the enthusiasm accompanying its discovery, it was easy enough to mistake advocacy as a *professional response* to presumably unmet social needs, with activism as a *political* response. Clearly and intentionally identifying advocacy with political action, a professor of social work has defined the advocate as "the professional who identifies with the victims of social problems and who pursues modification in social conditions"; and he has argued that the advocate "will need to have the professional dedication to take the risk and be political."[116] Needless to say, this interpretation has not gone unchallenged, and there is no indication that this is the meaning given it by most members of the legal profession where it originated in the first place.[117]

Paradoxically, its radical appearance notwithstanding, advocacy implies an essentially paternalistic attitude. Although he does not give it this interpretation, Edgar H. Schein, speaking of "role innovators," has this to say:

> These members of the profession accept its central or pivotal norms but try to redefine where, how, and on whom the profession is to be practiced. A strong theme in this group has been the concern for the ultimate client, who is the actual receiver of professional services but who may have little or no voice in the design of those services—the consumer, the low-income tenant, the welfare recipient, the

nonpaying charity case in the local hospital, the ghetto dweller. Thus, advocacy law and advocacy architecture are efforts by some lawyers and architects to provide services to clients who never saw themselves as clients, who did not realize that they were entitled to any voice in their own affairs, and who could not pay professional fees.[118]

The professional as advocate not only knows what is best for people but also has the advantage over political representatives of not being responsible to his clients as elected officials are responsible to their constituents. So the professional as advocate must fall back on the collective mandate given his profession by society. But in taking the generalized mandate theory seriously, advocate professionals should answer some serious questions. What will happen if things go wrong? To whom will the advocate professional be accountable? His clients, his peers, his employers, or only his own conscience? What would accountability imply? Would it imply making restitution? Risking censure or suspension of license? Dismissal from the job? Most of these questions have yet to be answered.

Advocacy as a professional response to unmet social needs and not as a substitute, in professional guise, for social action, has come to be accepted in the planning profession. This profession has understandably long been of interest to political science, for two reasons—first, because its clientele is never an individual person, and second, because its activities are clearly and intimately implicated in the public interest.[119] The plight of people displaced by urban renewal projects became a source of protest, but protest alone would never have brought about a solution in the public interest.[120] What makes possible a broadening of the meaning of public interest is the intervention of advocacy planners who bring the interests of the deprived groups into the planning process by giving them expert advice. The relationship between the expert-advocate, individual or firm, and the client organization has taken a variety of forms. Blecher, in an analysis of six demonstration programs, found that when the relationship followed the classical model of a strictly formal contract between professional and client, relations of the client group with public authorities were less conflictual than when the client organization tried to influence directly the technical aspects of the planning process.[121]

The most significant contribution of the advocacy role, or what the lawyers interestingly call "public interest work," is perhaps not its immediate payoffs to clients in need, but its bringing the profession's idealized model of public service somewhat closer to reality than it has been in the past. Nevertheless, the present extent and future promises of the advocacy role should not be overestimated. As a very thorough recent study of the legal profession concludes,

> The level of public interest work by those parts of the private bar that we observed was low; the delivered efforts of private firms represent only a small part

of the available energies of those firms. For the bar as a whole the response appears to be even smaller; indeed it appears to be infinitesimal. Certainly one cannot say that the bar as a whole has fashioned a public interest response unless some of the institutional definitions of professional responsibility are being affected by its efforts.[122]

Because it is dependent on government or foundation support which may be withdrawn, or because clients themselves may reject an advocate's help, the role is difficult to sustain. Nevertheless, as a new form of professional conduct, and if it is not misused, professional advocacy is quite in line with the realities of technological society. However, it should not be considered an alternative to either conventional or unconventional politics. Although in articulating and advocating client needs the professional puts them on a firmer knowledge base than would otherwise be the case, interest-group formation and pressure politics will continue to be primary ways to influence policy making and administration.

To predict the outcome of the contemporary ferment in the relationship between the professions and society is imprudent. There is only a thin line between politicization that leads to deprofessionalization of human services, on the one hand, and responsible involvement in those public issues that are the legitimate concern of the professions, on the other hand. Political awareness will make the professions perhaps more responsive to societal needs; but professionals must bring to the treatment of public issues professionally pertinent criteria of substance and conduct that warrant their being respected for their knowledge and skills rather than for the particular ideological predilections that may be the fashion of the moment. The winds of politics are moody and have a way of changing faster than professional responses to these winds.

THE CONSULTATIVE COMMONWEALTH

Rooted in the social and technological changes occasioned by the modern skill revolution, the consultative commonwealth does not denote a revolutionary state. On the contrary, the construct assumes that as a result of the prominence of old and new professions in policy making and the delivery of human services, consultative modes of interaction will be a pervasive feature of governance in the future society. Consultation is the most characteristic aspect of the relationships among professional skill specialists and between them and their clients. Consultation will not be the dominant process but will complement, supplement, and implement other governmental processes like democratic participation, bureaucratic organization, pluralistic bargaining, or oligarchic decision making.

It is because professionalization and deprofessionalization are mutually entailed that professionalization will not usher in the bureaucratic state of rulership through professional expertise, and deprofessionalization will not bring in the democratic state of governance through client participation. There will be both more bureaucratization and more democratization, but the skill revolution will inject professional ways of doing things into the emerging commonwealth. Although they are necessary, neither bureaucratic nor democratic techniques are sufficient to cope with the extraordinarily complex social and technological problems of the future. Consultation will be a necessary but also not sufficient condition of the future commonwealth.

In the real world of politics, consultation is contaminated by other social processes so that it can never occur in pure form. The consultative commonwealth is therefore not a political system in which men of knowledge or skill specialists have uncontested power to constitute a new ruling class. Rather, it is a system of government in which professional norms and modes of conduct are acknowledged components of individual and collective choice making, at the level both of policy and of administration. The construct assumes that insofar as familiar bureaucratic-hierarchical and participative-representational patterns continue, they will be permeated by consultative patterns. This is so because in the technological society, the ways of consultation are, on balance, well suited to the formulation and delivery of professionally based services. For consultation infuses professional expertise as well as client perspective into the policy process and the delivery of services.

Consultation as a form of interaction does not assume equality among all participants. It takes for granted that the participants are unequal precisely because the professional whose advice or service is sought is superior to the client in his area of competence. Were it otherwise, the whole notion of expertise and skill specialization would be meaningless. The inequality taken for granted is of course based on an authority of competence and not of position. The client may be superior or equal to the consultant in social status or organizational position, but for the purposes of consultation he is dependent on the consultant. But a political milieu reduces the status advantage that the professional normally has in his client relationships. Professionals cannot simply depend on their authority but may have to persuade their clients, especially if the clients are highly placed executive or legislative policy makers. Policy makers as clients do not stand in awe of professionals.

There are also limits to professional dominance at the humble end of government where the low-level bureaucratic professional encounters his clients. One of the paradoxes of professional practice is that the professional's reputation partly depends on his being evaluated, whether he likes it or not, by clients— that is, precisely by those persons least qualified technically to judge professional performance. The more that human services are extended to larger classes of people and become professionalized, the less are clients willing to be passive recipients of service, and the greater is their demand for high performance.[123] The professional's need for at least some client approval has always been a source of client control.[124]

It is in the nature of pluralistic processes to multiply channels of consultation, thereby introducing competition into the advisory function. As expert encounters expert, alternative solutions become political compromises that safeguard the commonwealth against the professional or personal biases of skill specialists.[125] What Rourke says of bureaucrats is equally applicable to professionals in political milieux: "In the case of advice, the power of bureaucrats is indirect, resting as it does upon their ability to persuade political officials that a certain course of action should be taken. Bureaucrats have influence only if politicians accept their advice."[126]

Constitutionally speaking, then, the consultative commonwealth is characterized by status ambiguity. In the classical professional-client model, the professional is in a superior and the client in a subordinate position. In the professional-colleague relationship, the actors appear to be in equal positions. And in the professional-organization relationship, the professional's position appears to be subordinate to that of the organizational supervisor. But in reality these constitutional relationships vary a good deal and may actually be reversed. Clients do have ways of controlling the professional; status jealousies among professionals interfere with mutual deference; and professionals in organizations have ways of gaining the upper hand. Especially in organizational settings in which the professional interacts simultaneously with clients, colleagues, and supervisors, ambiguities inherent in any one relationship will be confounded by the complexity of the total network in which all the actors are enmeshed.

The need to integrate specializations and subspecializations into a coherent professional service is best met through consultation. Neither market-type exchange mechanisms nor hierarchical modes are sufficient to coordinate diverse specialties. Status differences within and among the professions make nonconsultative ways of coordination problematical, for they ignore ambiguities in status relationships. On the one hand, the "superior" professional is expected to "direct" the work of subordinate personnel; but on the other hand, for some purposes the higher-skill specialist "depends" or "relies" on the lower-skill specialist, as physicians depend on nurses or university professors rely on librarians.[127]

Traditional solutions to the coordination of specialized services have been, first, to have professionals run their own affairs, as professors do in some universities; second, to turn coordination over to lay boards, as in primary or secondary education; and third, to create altogether new administrative professions, like the city manager or hospital administrator. All of these modes of coordination make implicit assumptions about status differentiation. By transcending formal social or bureaucratic status lines and organizational barriers, consultation facilitates the utilization of diverse knowledge and intelligence that otherwise would not be brought to bear on policy making or administration, including knowledge of what is politically feasible and attainable.

Consultation will not erase ambiguities in professional relationships because status differentiation is immanent in skill differentiation. Therefore, inter-professional bargaining and negotiations concerning jurisdictional matters will continue in the consultative commonwealth,[128] as will hierarchical forms of conflict resolution. This is likely to be so because, as Moore puts it, "authenticated professionals are scarcely more prone to rational and sensible compromises and reasonable innovations than others who occupy a privileged position."[129]

The consultative commonwealth will be circumscribed by political and economic processes that may but need not involve consultation. Many human services will continue to be rendered by occupations whose professionalization is more a distant aspiration than an early prospect. To expect that in the foreseeable future the two largest and most powerful institutional sectors of society—government and business—will be fully professionalized would be to burden the construct of the consultative commonwealth beyond its heuristic capability.[130] Government, in particular, will be guided by the politics of elections, group processes, and bureaucratic inertia. The continuing skill revolution will accentuate the professionalization of advice and services *in* government, which is something different from the professionalization *of* government. Increased sensitivity of professionals to their own position in society and to the nature of their relationships with clients as diverse as slum dwellers and high policy makers will make for more rather than less politics in the consultative commonwealth,[131] but technological developments and the delivery of human services become increasingly dependent on consultation as the linkage mechanism between democracy and bureaucracy.[132]

NOTES

1: COM-COM TECHNOLOGY AND POLITICAL BEHAVIOR

1. By "com-com technology" is meant the technology that links the computer to media of communication, especially to television. The interactive information utility discussed below is an instance of com-com technology.

2. See Alan F. Westin, ed., *Information Technology in a Democracy* (Cambridge: Harvard University Press, 1971).

3. See Irene Taviss, ed., *The Computer Impact* (Englewood Cliffs, N.J.: Prentice-Hall, 1970).

4. See Raymond A. Bauer, ed., *Social Indicators* (Cambridge: M.I.T. Press, 1966); and Eleanor B. Sheldon and Wilbert E. Moore, eds., *Indicators of Social Change* (New York: Russell Sage Foundation, 1968).

5. Simon Ramo, *Cure for Chaos* (New York: David McKay Company, 1969), p. x.

6. Theodore Roszak, *The Making of a Counter Culture* (Garden City, N.Y.: Doubleday and Company, Anchor Books, 1969), p. xiii.

7. See Heinz Eulau, "H. D. Laswell's Developmental Analysis," *Western Political Quarterly,* 11 (June 1958): 229–42.

8. Harold D. Lasswell, "The World Revolutionary Situation," in Carl J. Friedrich, ed., *Totalitarianism* (Cambridge: Harvard University Press, 1954), p. 360.

9. The etymology of "imputation" must be understood to appreciate the word's meaning. *Imputare,* the Latin verb, can be translated as "to bring into reckoning," while "reckon" is related to the German verb *rechnen,* which may mean, as does reckon, "to count, compute, calculate." Imputing something involves at least some "loose" calculation.

10. Alvin Toffler, *Future Shock* (New York: Bantam Books, 1970), p. 11.

11. For the proceedings of the conference see Harold Sackman and Norman Nie, eds., *The Information Utility and Social Choice* (Montvale, N.J.: American Federation of Information Processing Societies Press, 1970).

12. This is reported in a paper by Edwin B. Parker, "On-Line Polling and Voting," Harold Sackman and E. H. Boehm, eds., *Planning Community Information Utilities,* (Montvale, N.J.: American Federation of Information Processing Societies Press, 1972).

13. These problems are discussed in Robert A. Dunlop, "The Emerging Technology of Information Utilities," in Sackman and Nie, pp. 25–50.

14. Don K. Price, *The Scientific Estate* (New York: Oxford University Press, 1965), p. 84.

15. Price, p. 289, n. 2: "Simon Ramo, address at the University of California at Los Angeles, May 1, 1961 (mimeo). The idea was subsequently noted in the *Report of the American Assembly: 1962–63* (New York: Columbia University Press)."

16. Zbigniew Brzezinski, *Between Two Ages: America's Role in the Technetronic Era* (New York: Viking Press, 1970), p. 259.

17. Ibid.

18. See Heinz Eulau, "Some Potential Effects of the Information Utility on Political Decision-Makers and the Role of the Representative," in Sackman and Nie, pp. 187–216.

19. Edwin B. Parker, "Information Utilities and Mass Communication," in Sackman and Nie, p. 69.

20. Anthony Downs, *An Economic Theory of Democracy* (New York: Harper & Brothers, 1957), pp. 260–76.

21. See Chapter 2.

2: POTENTIAL EFFECTS OF THE INFORMATION UTILITY

1. Anthony Downs, *An Economic Theory of Democracy* (New York: Harper & Brothers, 1957), pp. 260–76.

2. Ibid., pp. 245–46.

3. Ibid., p. 88.

4. Ibid., p. 89.

5. Ibid.

6. Ibid.

7. Hanna F. Pitkin, ed., *Representation* (New York: Atherton Press, 1969), p. 20.

8. Kenneth F. Janda, "Democratic Theory and Legislative Behavior: A Study of Legislator-Constituency Relationships" (Ph.D. diss., Indiana University, 1961), pp. 169–70.

9. Edmund Burke, "Speech to the Electors of Bristol," *Works,* vol. 2 (n. p., 1774), p. 12.

10. Kenneth Prewitt and Heinz Eulau, "Political Matrix and Political Representation: Prolegomenon to a New Departure from an Old Problem," *American Political Science Review,* 66 (June, 1969): 427–41.

11. Kenneth Janda, "Providing Information to Congressmen," *Information Retrieval: Applications to Political Science* (Indianapolis: Bobbs-Merrill Company, 1968), pp. 184–220.

12. Harold D. Lasswell, "Current Studies of the Decision Process: Automation versus Creativity," *Western Political Quarterly* 8 (September, 1955): 339.

13. Karl W. Deutsch, *The Nerves of Government: Models of Political Communication and Control* (New York: Free Press, 1963), p. 161.

14. Charles E. Lindblom, *The Intelligence of Democracy: Decision-Making through Mutual Adjustment* (New York: Free Press, 1965), p. 171.

15. Mancur M. Olson, Jr., *The Logic of Collective Action* (Cambridge, Mass.: Harvard University Press, 1965), p. 114, n. 13.

3: TECHNOLOGY AND THE FEAR OF CIVILITY

1. The literature is enormous. For two works by political scientists, see Victor C. Ferkiss, *Technological Man: The Myth and the Reality* (New York: George Braziller, Inc., 1969), and Zbigniew Brzezinski, *Between Two Ages: America's Role in the Technetronic Era* (New York: Viking Press, 1970).

2. See, for instance, Charles A. Reich, *The Greening of America* (New York: Random House, 1970).

3. Don K. Price, *Government and Science* (New York: New York University Press, 1954), p. 27.

4. Carl Marcy, *Presidential Commissions* (New York: King's Crown Press, 1945), pp. 42–47, quoted in George T. Sulzner, "The Policy Process and the Uses of National Governmental Study Commissions," *Western Political Quarterly* 24 (September 1971): 439.

5. Lewis M. Branscomb, "Taming Technology," *Science* 171 (March 12, 1971): 974–75.

6. Ibid., 975.

7. Ibid.

8. Ibid.

9. Ibid., 975—76.

10. James Schlesinger, "Two-and-a-Half Cheers for Systems Analysis," in Alan F. Westin, ed., *Information Technology in a Democracy* (Cambridge, Mass.: Harvard University Press, 1971), p. 398.

11. Ibid.

12. B. F. Skinner, *Walden Two* (New York: Macmillan Co., 1948).

13. B. F. Skinner, "Some Issues Concerning the Control of Human Behavior," in Jack D. Douglas, ed., *The Technological Threat* (Englewood Cliffs, N.J.: Prentice-Hall, Inc.), p. 123.

14. Ibid., p. 124.

15. Ibid., p. 128.

16. Ibid., p. 129.

17. Ibid., p. 130.

18. Ibid., p. 131.

19. Ibid.

20. Ibid.

21. See Charles E. Lindblom, *The Intelligence of Democracy* (New York: Free Press, 1965).

22. Published in 1629. See Francis Bacon, *The Advancement of Learning and New Atlantis* (Oxford: Clarendon Press, 1974).

23. Howard B. White, "Francis Bacon," in Leo Strauss and Joseph Cropsey, eds., *History of Political Philosophy* (Chicago: Rand McNally & Company, 1963), p. 337.

24. See Donald A. Strickland, *Scientists in Politics: The Atomic Scientists Movement, 1945—46* (Lafayette, Ind.: Purdue University Studies, 1968).

25. *Revolution for the Hell of It* (New York: Simon & Schuster, Inc., Pocket Books, 1970).

26. Theodore Roszak, *The Making of a Counter Culture* (Garden City, N.Y.: Doubleday & Co., Anchor Books, 1969), p. 2.

27. Ibid., pp. 4—5.

28. Ibid., pp. 13—14.

29. Ibid., p. 148.

30. Ibid., p. 149.

31. Ibid., pp. 149—150.

32. Ibid., pp. 266—267.

33. Philip Selznick, *TVA and the Grass Roots* (Berkeley: University of California Press, 1949), p. 13.

34. Bennett W. Berger, "Strategies for Radical Social Change," *Social Policy* 1 (November/December 1970): 18—19.

35. Stanley Aronowitz, "Strategies for Radical Social Change," *Social Policy,* 1 (November/December 1970): 12.

4: POLITICS AND EDUCATION

1. Heinz Eulau, "Political Science: I," in Bert F. Hoselitz, ed., *A Reader's Guide to the Social Sciences,* rev. ed. (New York: The Free Press, 1970), p. 132. I should say that this was written in 1956 and first published in 1959.

2. Ibid., p. 131.

3. I could cite here just as well the late V. O. Key's chapter on "The Educational System" in *Public Opinion and American Democracy* (New York: Alfred A. Knopf, 1961), pp. 315—343. Key

orders his variables in the same way as Almond and Verba do. But I think both his premises and inferences are different—in fact inconsistent with his data presentation. Almond and Verba, on the other hand, are highly consistent and interpret their findings within the contours of the underlying model.

4. Gabriel A. Almond and Sidney Verba, *The Civic Culture: Political Attitudes and Democracy in Five Nations* (Princeton, N.J.: Princeton University Press, 1963), p. 379.

5. Ibid., p. 502.

6. Ibid., p. 503.

7. It is amusing, and I think ironic, that the author of a recent text in political theory entitles one of his chapters "The Aristotelian Bridge: Aristotle, Lipset, Almond." See William T. Bluhm, *Theories of the Political System* (Englewood Cliffs, N.J.: Prentice-Hall, 1965).

8. Robert E. Ward, "Japan: The Continuity of Modernization," in Lucian W. Pye and Sidney Verba, eds. *Political Culture and Political Development* (Princeton, N.J.: Princeton University Press, 1965), p. 29.

9. Lucian W. Pye, *Politics, Personality, and Nation Building: Burma's Search for Identity* (New Haven: Yale University Press, 1962), p. 220.

10. Robert T. Holt and John E. Turner, *The Political Basis of Economic Development* (Princeton, N.J.: D. Van Nostrand Company, 1966), p. 270.

11. John Stuart Mill, *On Liberty,* R. B. McCallum, ed. (Oxford: Basil Blackwell, 1947), p. 95.

12. Ernest Barker, *Principles of Social and Political Theory* (Oxford: At the Clarendon Press, 1951), p. 277.

13. Charles E. Merriam, *The Making of Citizens: A Comparative Study of Methods of Civic Training* (Chicago: University of Chicago Press, 1931), p. x.

14. Ibid., pp. x–xi.

15. Charles E. Merriam, *Systematic Politics* (Chicago: University of Chicago Press, 1945), pp. 100–101.

16. Nicholas A. Masters, Robert H. Salisbury, and Thomas H. Eliot, *State Politics and the Public Schools: An Exploratory Analysis* (New York: Alfred A. Knopf, 1964).

17. Harmon Zeigler, *The Political Life of American Teachers* (Englewood Cliffs, N.J.: Prentice-Hall, 1967).

18. Edgar Litt, *The Public Vocational University: Captive Knowledge and Public Power* (New York: Holt, Rinehart and Winston, 1969).

19. Which explains, perhaps, why I find much of virtue in Emile Durkheim's *Moral Education,* Everett K. Wilson, ed. (New York: The Free Press, 1961).

5: POLITICAL NORMS IN EDUCATIONAL POLICY MAKING

1. See, for instance, Anthony Downs, *An Economic Theory of Democracy* (New York: Harper & Row, 1957); James M. Buchanan and Gordon Tullock, *The Calculus of Consent* (Ann Arbor: University of Michigan Press, 1962); Mancur Olson, Jr., *The Logic of Collective Action: Public Goods and the Theory of Groups* (Cambridge, Mass.: Harvard University Press, 1965); R. L. Curry, Jr., and L. L. Wade, *A Theory of Political Exchange: Economic Reasoning in Political Analysis* (Englewood Cliffs, N.J.: Prentice-Hall, 1968).

2. William C. Mitchell, "The Ambivalent Social Status of the American Politician," *Western Political Quarterly* 12 (September 1959): 683–98; and "Occupational Role Strains: The American Elective Public Official," *Administrative Science Quarterly* 3 (September 1958): 219–28.

3. The leading work still is John C. Wahlke et al., *The Legislative System: Explorations in Legislative Behavior* (New York: John Wiley & Sons, 1962). See also Roger H. Davidson, *The Role of the Congressman* (New York: Pegasus, 1969).

4. John C. Wahlke et al., "American State Legislators' Role Orientations toward Pressure Groups," *Journal of Politics* 22 (May 1960): 203–27; Betty H. Zisk, Heinz Eulau, and Kenneth Prewitt, "City Councilmen and the Group Struggle: A Typology of Role Orientations," *Journal of Politics* 27 (August 1965): 618–45; Lester W. Milbrath, *The Washington Lobbyists* (Chicago: Rand McNally, 1963); Harmon Zeigler and Michael Baer, *Lobbying: Interaction and Influence in American State Legislatures* (Belmont, Calif.: Wadsworth, 1969).

5. Donald R. Matthews, "The Folkways of the Senate," *U.S. Senators and Their World* (Chapel Hill: University of North Carolina Press, 1960), pp. 92–117; Wahlke et al., "Rules of the Game," *The Legislative System,* pp. 141–69; Allan Kornberg, "Rules of the Game in the Canadian House of Commons," *Journal of Politics* 26 (May 1964): 358–80; Ralph K. Huitt, "The Morse Committee Assignment Controversy: A Study in Senate Norms," *American Political Science Review* 51 (June 1957): 313–29.

6. Samuel C. Patterson, "Patterns of Interpersonal Relations in a State Legislative Group: The Wisconsin Assembly," *Public Opinion Quarterly* 23 (Spring 1959): 101–10; Wayne L. Francis, "Influence and Interaction in a State Legislative Body," *American Political Science Review* 56 (December 1962): 953–60; Alan Fiellin, "The Function of Informal Groups in Legislative Institutions," *Journal of Politics* 24 (February 1962): 72–91.

7. James D. Barber, *The Lawmakers: Recruitment and Adaptation to Legislative Life* (New Haven, Conn.: Yale University Press, 1965); Richard F. Fenno, Jr., *The Power of the Purse: Appropriations Politics in Congress* (Boston: Little, Brown & Co., 1966); Ralph K. Huitt and Robert L. Peabody, *Congress: Two Decades of Analysis* (New York: Harper & Row, 1969).

8. William Buchanan et al., "The Legislator as Specialist," *Western Political Quarterly* 13 (September 1960): 636–51; Heinz Eulau, "Bases of Authority in Legislative Bodies: A Comparative Analysis," *Administrative Science Quarterly* 7 (December 1962): 309–21; Nelson W. Polsby et al., "The Growth of the Seniority System in the U.S. House of Representatives," *American Political Science Review* 63 (September 1969): 787–807.

9. The classic and still one of the best of these case studies is Stephen K. Bailey, *Congress Makes a Law: The Story Behind the Employment Act of 1946* (New York: Columbia University Press, 1950); among more recent studies, see Raymond A. Bauer, Ithiel de Sola Pool, and Lewis A. Dexter, *American Business and Public Policy: The Politics of Foreign Trade* (New York: Atherton Press, 1963).

10. See, for instance, Nicholas A. Masters, Robert H. Salisbury, and Thomas H. Eliot, *State Politics and the Public Schools: An Exploratory Analysis* (New York: Alfred Knopf, 1964); Edgar Litt, *The Public Vocational University: Captive Knowledge and Public Power* (New York: Holt, Rinehart & Winston, 1969).

11. Heinz Eulau and Harold Quinley, *American State Officials' Attitudes Toward Higher Education* (New York: McGraw-Hill Book Co., 1970) is a condensed version of the survey.

12. Ten intensive interviews were also conducted in the Congress by Dr. Robert L. Peabody. Some excerpts were used earlier in this paper.

13. See Heinz Eulau et al., "The Role of the Representative," *American Political Science Review* 53 (September 1959): 742–56; Kenneth Prewitt and Heinz Eulau, "Political Matrix and Political Representation," *American Political Science Review* 63 (June 1969): 427–41.

14. Jack L. Walker, "The Diffusion of Innovations among the American States," *American Political Science Review* 63 (September 1969): 880–99; see also Wayne L. Francis, *Legislative Issues in the Fifty States: A Comparative Analysis* (Chicago: Rand McNally, 1967).

7: SKILL REVOLUTION AND CONSULTATIVE COMMONWEALTH

1. By "technological society" I mean a society in which not only agricultural and industrial production have been automated, computerized, and otherwise rationalized, but one in which the provision of human services also is increasingly subject to technological innovation. I prefer this expression to "postindustrial society" because the latter does not really convey a meaning of the

direction of change. A technological society need not be "technocratic." The construct of "consultative commonwealth" assumes the technologization (and professionalization) of the human services but not rule by technologists. See Victor C. Ferkiss, *Technological Man: The Myth and the Reality* (New York: George Braziller, 1969), or Zbigniew Brzezinski, *Between Two Ages: America's Role in the Technetronic Era* (New York: Viking Press, 1970).

2. "Consultative" is related to consult and consultation. These words derive from the Latin *consultare,* which has at least three behavior-relevant meanings. All of these meanings define, etymologically, the consultative commonwealth. First, depending on the context in which it is used, *consultare* can be translated as consider, deliberate, cogitate, reflect, think over, advise with, take advice from, and so on. The variety of these meanings is less helpful, however, than the meanings of the more primitive Latin verb *consulere,* which directly calls attention to the reciprocal character of the consulting relationship. On the one hand, *consulere* means to ask, question, or examine; on the other hand, it means to give counsel. The reciprocity appears even more strongly in the German translation of *consulere* where it simultaneously means to ask someone (*jemanden befragen*) and to advise someone (*jemanden beraten*).

To seek, give, or take advice is hardly the only property of professional behavior. Interestingly, *consultare* refers to a second family of meanings that define the consulting relationship. In some contexts, *consultare* is used as synonym for *curare*—to care for or worry about—and for *prospicere*—to provide for. In this usage, then, both an empathetic and a providential aspect of consultation are emphasized.

Thirdly, the related adjective *consultus*—one who is consulted—may be used as a synonym for *intellegens, peritus,* or *eruditus*—intelligent, expert, and learned; and the process to which consultus applies is supposed to be *diligens* or *accuratus*—careful or accurate.

In combination, the different meanings and uses of *consultare* yield a comprehensive profile of the consultative relationship. The relationship is entered voluntarily for the purpose of deliberation or consideration because one party, the seeker of advice, is ignorant or in need of help, while the other party, the consultant, is a skilled or learned person who gives advice diligently and intelligently. The consultant, however, is not just an expert but also a compassionate person who cares for and worries about the matter brought to him for counsel, and he has the gift of accurate diagnosis and wise prognosis.

3. See Harold D. Lasswell, "The Garrison State and Specialists on Violence," in *The Analysis of Political Behavior: An Empirical Approach* (New York: Oxford University Press, 1948), pp. 146–57.

4. See Warren G. Bennis and Philip E. Slater, *The Temporary Society* (New York: Harper and Row, 1969). In this utopia, problem solving by strangers with diverse professional skills is expected to occur through organic rather than mechanical means of interaction; the executive becomes a coordinator who mediates among task forces; and "people will be evaluated not according to rank but according to skill and professional training. . . . Adaptive, problem-solving temporary systems of diverse specialists linked together by coordinating and task-evaluating executive specialists in an organic flux—this is the organization form that will gradually replace bureaucracy as we know it" (p. 74). Bennis's view of democracy, though he does not seem to know it, is anarcho-syndicalist: " . . . democracy seeks no new stability, no end point; it is purposeless, save that it purports to ensure perpetual transition, constant alteration, ceaseless instability. . . . Democracy and our new professional men identify primarily with the adaptive process, not the establishment." (p. 12).

5. For a discussion of "developmental constructs," see Heinz Eulau, "H. D. Lasswell's Developmental Analysis," in *Micro-Macro Political Analysis: Accents of Inquiry* (Chicago: Aldine Publishing Company, 1969), p. 105–18.

6. The classical work on the professions remains A. M. Carr-Saunders and P. A. Wilson, *The Professions* (Oxford: The Clarendon Press, 1933). See also these authors' article, "Professions," in *Encyclopedia of the Social Sciences,* vol. 12 (New York: Macmillan Company, 1934), pp. 476–80. For a contemporary overview, see Kenneth S. Lynn, ed., *The Professions in America* (Boston: Beacon Press, 1965).

7. Emile Durkheim, *The Division of Labor in Society,* trans. George Simpson (Glencoe, Ill.: The Free Press, 1960). First Published in 1893.

8. Harold D. Lasswell, "Skill Politics and Skill Revolution," in Lasswell, *Analysis of Political Behavior,* pp. 133–45, at 135.

9. See Nicholas De Witt, *Education and Professional Employment in the U.S.S.R.* (Washington, D.C.: National Science Foundation, 1961), pp. 207–545; George Fischer, *The Soviet System and Modern Society* (New York: Atherton Press, 1968); for long-term transformations, see some of the essays in Cyril E. Black, ed., *The Transformation of Russian Society* (Cambridge: Harvard University Press, 1960); Milton C. Lodge, *Soviet Elite Attitudes Since Stalin* (Columbus, Ohio: Charles E. Merrill Publishing Company, 1969).

10. Peter M. Blau and Otis Dudley Duncan, *The American Occupational Structure* (New York: John Wiley & Sons, 1967); Richard H. Hall, *Occupations and the Social Structure* (Englewood Cliffs, N.J.: Prentice-Hall, 1969).

11. See Harold D. Lasswell, Daniel Lerner, and C. Easton Rothwell, *The Comparative Study of Elites* (Stanford: Stanford University Press, 1952).

12. See, for instance, John Kenneth Galbraith, *The New Industrial State* (Boston: Houghton Mifflin Company, 1967); Michael Young, *The Rise of the Meritocracy, 1870–2033* (London: Thames and Hudson, 1958). For an earlier example of this genre, see James Burnham, *The Managerial Revolution* (New York: The John Day Company, 1941).

13. Frederick C. Mosher, *Democracy and the Public Service* (New York: Oxford University Press, 1968). This is not to say that I disagree with Mosher's appraisal that "the emergence of the professions [has] revolutionized the precepts and practices of public employment" (p. 123). By turning over the recruitment, training and accreditation of skilled employees to the professions and the universities, current practices "are challenging, modifying, or overturning the most central— and most cherished—principles associated with civil service reform . . . " (p. 124). It is unlikely, Mosher concludes, "that the trend toward professionalism in or outside government will soon be reversed or even slowed" (pp. 132–33).

14. "The leadership of the new society will rest," writes Daniel Bell, "not with the businessmen or corporations as we know them . . . , but with the research corporations, the industrial laboratories, the experimental stations, and the universities." Daniel Bell, "Notes on Post-Industrial Society I," *The Public Interest* 6 (Winter, 1967): 27.

15. Among the few exceptions are Herbert Kaufman, *The Forest Ranger: A Study in Administrative Behavior* (Baltimore: Johns Hopkins Press, 1960); Bernard C. Cohen, *The Press and Foreign Policy* (Princeton: Princeton University Press, 1963); Heinz Eulau and John D. Sprague, *Lawyers in Politics: A Study in Professional Convergence* (Indianapolis: The Bobbs Merrill Company, 1964); Robert C. Wood, "Scientists and Politics: The Rise of an Apolitical Elite," in *Scientists and National Policy-Making,* eds. Robert Gilpin and Christopher Wright (New York: Columbia University Press, 1964), pp. 41–72; Arnold A. Rogow, *The Psychiatrists* (New York: G. P. Putnam's Sons, 1970); Harmon Zeigler, *The Political World of the High School Teacher* (Eugene, Oregon: Center for the Advanced Study of Educational Administration, 1966); Morris Janowitz, *The Professional Soldier: A Social and Political Portrait,* new ed. (New York: The Free Press, 1971); Everett C. Ladd, Jr. and Seymour Martin Lipset, "Politics of Academic Natural Scientists and Engineers," *Science* 176 (June 9, 1972): 1091–1100.

16. See Corinne Lathrop Gilb, *Hidden Hierarchies: The Professions and Government* (New York: Harper and Row, 1966); and Martin Mayer, *The Lawyers* (New York: Harper and Row, 1968); Eliot Freidson, *Profession of Medicine* (New York: Dodd, Mead, 1970).

17. The pioneering study is Oliver Garceau, *The Political Life of the American Medical Association* (Cambridge: Harvard University Press, 1941); see also Stanley Kelley, Jr., *Professional Public Relations and Political Power* (Baltimore: Johns Hopkins Press, 1956); Harry Eckstein, *Pressure Group Politics: The Case of the British Medical Association* (Stanford: Stanford University Press, 1960); Joel B. Grossman, *Lawyers and Judges: The ABA and the Politics of Judicial Selection* (New York: John Wiley & Sons, 1965); Samuel P. Huntington, *The Soldier and the State* (Cambridge: Harvard University Press, 1957).

18. See Donald R. Matthews, *The Social Background of Political Decision-Makers* (New York: Doubleday & Company, 1954). See also Dwaine Marvick, ed., *Political Decision-Makers: Recruitment and Performance* (New York: The Free Press, 1961); Mattei Dogan and Stein Rokkan,

eds., *Quantitative Ecological Analysis in the Social Sciences* (Cambridge: MIT Press, 1969).

19. For an appraisal, see Lewis J. Edinger, "Political Science and Political Biography: Reflections on the Study of Leadership," *Journal of Politics* 26 (May and August, 1964): 423–34, 648–76. For a recent reassertion, see Fred I. Greenstein, *Personality and Politics* (Chicago: Markham Publishing Company, 1969).

20. On emergence, see Ernest Nagel, *The Structure of Science* (New York: Harcourt, Brace & World, 1961), p. 366–80.

21. See Albert J. Reiss, Jr., *Occupations and Social Status* (New York: The Free Press, 1961). For measurement aspects, see John P. Robinson et al., *Measures of Occupational Attitudes and Occupational Characteristics* (Ann Arbor: Survey Research Center, Institute for Social Research, University of Michigan, 1967). For a broad overview, see Joseph Ben-David, "Professions in the Class System of Present-Day Societies: A Trend Report and Bibliography," *Current Sociology* 12 (1963–4): 247–330.

22. Amitai Etzioni, ed., *The Semi-Professions and Their Organization: Teachers, Nurses, Social Workers* (New York: The Free Press, 1969).

23. See William Mitchell, "The Ambivalent Social Status of the American Politician," *Western Political Quarterly* 12 (September, 1959): 683–98.

24. See, for instance, Daniel Bell, ed., *Toward the Year 2000: Work in Progress* (Boston: Beacon Press, 1969).

25. The polarity principle is explicated in the writings of the philosopher Morris R. Cohen. See, for instance, *Studies in Philosophy and Science* (New York: Henry Holt and Company, 1949), pp. 11–13: "The principle of polarity is suggested by the phenomena of magnetism where north and south pole are always distinct, opposed, yet inseparable. We can see it in general physics where there is no action without reaction, no force or cause of change without inertia or resistance. In biology the life of every organism involves action and reaction with an environment. There is no growth without decay. . . . This suggests a supplement to the principle of causality. Not only must every natural event have a cause which determines that it should happen, but the cause must be opposed by some factor which prevents it from producing any greater effect than it actually does. . . . The principle of polarity, of necessary opposition in all determinate effects, thus becomes a heuristic principle directing our inquiry. . . . Yet the principle of polarity is not the same as that of the Hegelian dialectic. . . . "

26. Robert Boguslaw, *The New Utopians: A Study of System Design and Social Change* (Englewood Cliffs, N.J.: Prentice-Hall, 1965), p. 43, puts it nicely: "An applied scientist is a scientist who has had his hair cut." For further aspects of the problem, see Bernard Barber and Walter Hirsch, eds., *The Sociology of Science* (New York: The Free Press, 1962), as against Alvin W. Gouldner and S. M. Miller, eds., *Applied Sociology: Opportunities and Problems* (New York: The Free Press, 1965).

27. "The client comes to the professional because he has met a problem which he cannot himself handle." Everett C. Hughes, *Men and Their Work* (Glencoe: The Free Press, 1958), p. 141.

28. See Renee C. Fox, "Training for Uncertainty," in Mark Abrahamson, ed., *The Professional in the Organization* (Chicago: Rand McNally & Company, 1967), pp. 20–24. See also Renee C. Fox, *Experiment Perilous* (Glencoe: The Free Press, 1959).

29. The best discussion of what is meant by a "problematic situation" is still John Dewey, *Logic: The Theory of Inquiry* (New York: Henry Holt & Company, 1938).

30. The literature on America's "unsolved problems" is legion, but few works treat the matter from the perspective of the professions. But see: Harold L. Wilensky and Charles N. Lebeaux, *Industrial Society and Social Welfare* (New York: The Free Press, 1965); Eli Ginzberg, with Miriam Ostow, *Men, Money, and Medicine* (New York: Columbia University Press, 1969); F. Raymond Marks, with Kirk Leswing and Barbara A. Fortinsky, *The Lawyer, The Public, and Professional Responsibility* (Chicago: American Bar Foundation, 1972); Rosemary Stevens, *American Medicine and the Public Interest* (New Haven: Yale University Press, 1971); James Q. Wilson, *Varieties of Police Behavior* (Cambridge: Harvard University Press, 1968); Heinz Eulau and Harold Quinley, *State Officials and Higher Education* (New York: McGraw-Hill Book Company, 1970).

31. An early and still one of the best arguments in this regard is T. H. Marshall, "The Recent History of Professionalism in Relation to Social Structure and Social Policy," in T. H. Marshall, *Class, Citizenship, and Social Development* (Garden City, N.Y.: Doubleday Anchor Books, 1965), pp. 159–79. The essay was first published in 1939.

32. Market regulation of human services is proposed by Milton Friedman, *Capitalism and Freedom* (Chicago: University of Chicago Press, 1962), pp. 137–60.

33. See Murray Edelman, *Politics as Symbolic Action: Mass Arousal and Quiescence* (Chicago: Markham Publishing Company, 1971).

34. As Harold L. Wilensky points out, "While there may be a general tendency for occupations to seek professional status, remarkably few of the thousands of occupations in modern society attain it." See, "The Professionalization of Everyone?" *American Journal of Sociology* 70 (September, 1964): quotation is from p. 141.

35. As William J. Goode observes, "the occupational structure of industrial society is not becoming generally more professionalized, even though a higher percentage of the labor force is in occupations that enjoy higher prestige rankings and income and that call themselves 'professions'." See "The Theoretical Limits of Professionalization," in Etzioni, ed., *Semi-Professions*, p. 267.

36. There is a large literature on the consequences of technological change. Some of this literature is highly sensational; but see the MIT "Report of the Study of Critical Environmental Problems," *Man's Impact on the Global Environment* (Cambridge: MIT Press, 1970); William E. Ewald, Jr., ed., *Environment and Change: The Next Fifty Years* (Bloomington: Indiana University Press, 1968); Harrison Brown, *The Challenge of Man's Future* (New York: The Viking Press, 1954); William W. Brickman and Stanley Lehrer, eds., *Automation, Education and Human Values* (New York: Thomas Y. Crowell, 1966); Albert Teich, ed., *Technology and Man's Future* (New York: St. Martin's Press, 1972).

37. Howard M. Vollmer and Donald L. Mills, *Professionalization* (Englewood Cliffs, N.J.: Prentice-Hall, 1966), p. viii, differentiate between professionalism and professionalization, as follows: "Professionalism as an ideology may induce members of many occupational groups to strive to become professional, but at the same time, we can see that many occupational groups that express the ideology of professionalism in reality may not be very advanced in regard to professionalization. Professionalism may be a necessary constituent of professionalization, but professionalism is not a sufficient cause for the entire professionalization process."

38. See Harold L. Wilensky, *Organizational Intelligence: Knowledge and Policy in Government and Industry* (New York: Basic Books, 1967); Don K. Price, *The Scientific Estate* (New York: Oxford University Press, 1965).

39. Wilensky, "The Professionalization of Everyone?" p. 138, comes to a similar minimal set of criteria: "(1) the job of the professional is *technical*—based on systematic knowledge or doctrine acquired only through long prescribed training, (2) The professional man adheres to a set of professional norms."

40. See Frank Bowles and Frank A. DeCosta, *Between Two Worlds: A Profile of Negro Higher Education* (New York: McGraw-Hill Book Company, 1971); James L. Curtis, *Blacks, Medical Schools, and Society* (Ann Arbor: University of Michigan Press, 1971); Cynthia Fuchs Epstein *Woman's Place: Options and Limits of Professional Careers* (Berkeley: University of California Press, 1970).

41. See Piet Thoenes, *The Elite in the Welfare State* (New York: The Free Press, 1966).

42. For a balanced view, see Victor A. Thompson, *Bureaucracy and Innovation* (University, Alabama: University of Alabama Press, 1969).

43. For similar optimistic estimates of the future, see Amitai Etzioni, *The Active Society* (New York: The Free Press, 1968); and Warren Breed, *The Self-Guiding Society* (New York: The Free Press, 1971).

44. Hughes, *Men and Their Work*, p. 85.

45. See, for instance, Robert E. Lane, "The Decline of Politics and Ideology in a Knowledgeable Society," *American Sociological Review* 31 (October, 1966): 649–62.

46. Hughes, *Men and Their Work*, p. 54.

47. This is reinforced by monopolistic practice, the prestige of the profession as a whole and the imputation of competence to the individual consultant. As Eliot Freidson, *Professional Dominance: The Social Structure of Medical Care* (New York: Atherton Press, 1970), pp. 120–21, points out, this doctrine is unsatisfactory because it allows the consultant "to rest on the authority of his professional status without having to try to present persuasive evidence to the client that his findings and advice are correct."

48. See Aaron I. Able, ed., *American Catholic Thought on Social Questions* (Indianapolis: The Bobbs-Merrill Company, 1968).

49. See Edgar H. Schein, *Professional Education: Some New Directions* (New York: McGraw-Hill Book Company, 1972).

50. Hughes, *Men and Their Work,* p. 83.

51. See Jerome E. Carlin, *Lawyers on Their Own* (New Brunswick: Rutgers University Press, 1962); Jack Ladinsky, "Careers of Lawyers, Law Practice, and Legal Institutions," *American Sociological Review* 28 (February 1963): 47–54; Erwin O. Smigel, *The Wall Street Lawyer* (New York: The Free Press, 1964).

52. Harry Specht, "The Deprofessionalization of Social Work," *Social Work* 17 (March, 1972); quotation is on p. 6.

53. Although this theme has much agitated the academic professions in recent years, it is not especially new. Alexander H. Leighton, *Human Relations in a Changing World* (New York: E. P. Dutton & Company, 1949) p. 128, reports a Washington saying that "the administrator uses social science the way a drunk uses a lamppost, for support rather than illumination." See especially Gene M. Lyons, *The Uneasy Partnership: Social Science and the Federal Government in the Twentieth Century* (New York: Russell Sage Foundation, 1969).

54. Michael H. Moskow and Kenneth McLennan, "Teacher Negotiations and School Decentralization," in Henry M. Levin, ed., *Community Control of Schools* (Washington, D.C.: The Brookings Institution, 1970), pp. 191–215.

55. For a variety of perspectives, see Barney G. Glaser, ed., *Organizational Careers: A Sourcebook for Theory* (Chicago: Aldine Publishing Company, 1968). See also F. William Howton, *Functionaries* (Chicago: Quadrangle Books, 1969).

56. By 1962, it was possible to speak of a "knowledge industry," so pervasive had knowledge making become in the American economy. See Fritz Machlup, *The Production and Distribution of Knowledge in the United States* (Princeton: Princeton University Press, 1962). Also D. N. Chorafas, *The Knowledge Revolution: An Analysis of the International Brain Market* (New York: McGraw-Hill Book Company, 1968).

57. Robert L. Peabody, *Organizational Authority* (New York: Atherton Press, 1964), pp. 1–43.

58. See Harold L. Wilensky, *Intellectuals in Labor Unions* (Glencoe: The Free Press, 1956); William Kornhauser, *Scientists in Industry: Conflict and Accommodation* (Berkeley: University of California Press, 1962); Barney G. Glaser, *Organizational Scientists: Their Professional Careers* (Indianapolis: The Bobbs-Merrill Company, 1964); Warren O. Hagstrom, *The Scientific Community* (New York: Basic Books, 1965); Spencer Klaw, *The New Brahmins: Scientific Life in America* (New York: William Morrow & Company, 1968); Walter Hirsch, *Scientists in American Society* (New York: Random House, 1968).

59. A president-elect of the American Chemical Society once complained that the first loyalty of chemists, seventy per cent of whom are employed in industry, is to their employers. He felt that for the chemist to discharge his responsibility to society, he must have a "professional atmosphere where [he] will identify with his profession rather than his employer." *Science* 175 (February 4, 1972); quotation is on p. 501.

60. Logan Wilson, "Disjunctive Processes in an Academic Milieu," in Edward A. Tiryakian, ed., *Sociological Theory, Values, and Sociocultural Change,* (New York: The Free Press, 1963), p. 293.

61. See Dwaine Marvick, *Career Perspectives in a Bureaucratic Setting* (Ann Arbor: University of Michigan Press, 1954), chapter 4. See also Alvin W. Gouldner, "Cosmopolitans and

Locals: Toward an Analysis of Latent Social Roles," *Administrative Science Quarterly* 2 (December, 1957): 281–306, and 2 (March, 1958): 444–80.

62. Francis E. Rourke, *Bureaucracy, Politics and Public Policy* (Boston: Little, Brown & Company, 1969), p. 105. Because he sees professionalism in government as a political force, yet insists that "the importance of preserving the independence and integrity of certain kinds of expertise in government is thus very great," Rourke concludes that "the need for professional autonomy begins to assert itself in all phases of bureaucratic policy making" (p. 110). Rourke concedes that professionals are no more immune from political pressure than other public officials and suggests that public policy making in bureaucratic settings "becomes in effect a mixed system of politics and professionalism" (p. 111).

63. Max Weber, *The Theory of Social and Economic Organization* (New York: Oxford University Press, 1947), pp. 329–41.

64. Wilensky, "Professionalization," p. 150. T. H. Marshall, *Class Citizenship*, p. 171, articulated the same idea as early as 1939 when he wrote that in modern democratic societies "State and professions are being assimilated to one another. This is not happening through the absorption of the professions by the State, but by both of them moving from opposite directions to meet in a middle position."

65. Talcott Parsons, "The Professions and Social Structure," in *Essays in Sociological Theory* (Glencoe, Ill.: The Free Press, 1954), pp. 34–49.

66. Freidson, *Professional Dominance*, p. 211. This is Freidson's central argument in analyzing professional dominance and the ordering of the health services; see especially pp. 127–64.

67. There may be more than meets the eye in all this, for it has also been suggested that professional authority, in addition to being based on knowledge and competence, "does rest to some extent on tradition," and "to some degree the professional's authority *is* charismatic. . . ." See Nina Toren, "Semi-Professionalism and Social Work: A Theoretical Perspective," in Etzioni, ed., *The Semi-Professions and Their Organization*, p. 152.

68. See, for instance, Peter Blau, *The Dynamics of Bureaucracy* (Chicago: University of Chicago Press, 1959); Victor Thompson, *Modern Organization* (New York: Alfred A. Knopf, 1961).

69. See Harmon Zeigler, *The Political Life of American Teachers* (Englewood Cliffs, N.J.: Prentice-Hall, 1967); Joseph W. Gambino, "Faculty Unionism: From Theory to Practice," *"Industrial Relations* 11 (February, 1972): 1–17.

70. Deborah Shapley, "Unionization: Scientists, Engineers Mull over One Alternative," *Science* 176 (May 12, 1972): 618–21, at 618.

71. See David W. Ewing, *The Managerial Mind* (New York: The Free Press, 1964); William H. Whyte, Jr., *The Organization Man* (Garden City, N.Y.: Doubleday Anchor Books, 1956); Roy Lewis and Rosemary Stewart, *The Managers: A New Examination of the English, German and American Executive* (New York: Mentor Books, 1961).

72. See Sanford H. Kadish, "The Theory of the Profession and its Predicament," *AAUP Bulletin* 58 (June, 1972): 120–25; Seymour Martin Lipset, "The Politics of Academia," in David C. Nichols, ed., *Perspectives on Campus Tensions* (Washington, D.C.: American Council on Education, 1970), pp. 85–118.

73. Everett C. Hughes, "Psychology: Science and/or Profession," *The American Psychologist* 7 (August, 1952): 441–43; Talcott Parsons, "Some Problems Confronting Sociology as a Profession," *American Sociological Review* 24 (August, 1959): 547–559.

74. Eliot Freidson, "The Impurity of Professional Authority," in Howard S. Becker et al., eds., *Institutions and the Person* (Chicago: Aldine Publishing Company, 1968), p. 26, points out that if this is so, it suggests an "unemphasized point, namely, that the type of influence or authority exerted by the professional on his clients must be quite different from that exerted by the scientist on his colleagues—that professional and scientific 'authority' are different even though profession and science are both characterized by special technical competence."

75. Of course, professional associations like the American Bar Association or the American Medical Association are also devoted to the promotion of knowledge by way of learned meetings and

journals. In turn, purely scientific societies share some of the characteristics of the professional associations. This is precisely the reason why the distinction between science and profession is at best of limited analytic value.

76. Wilensky, "Professionalization," p. 149, also remarks that "the tacit component of their knowledge base is a seldom-recognized cause of the tenacious conservatism of the established professions."

77. Jerome E. Carlin, *Lawyers' Ethics: A Survey of the New York City Bar* (New York: Russell Sage Foundation, 1966), p. 170, estimates that "only about 2 per cent of the lawyers who violate generally accepted ethical norms are processed, and fewer than 0.2 per cent are officially sanctioned." If lawyers are so reluctant to enforce their ethics, other professions are likely to be even more lax.

78. See Gilb, *Hidden Hierarchies,* pp. 117–28. Gilb reports that in 1960 less than half of attorneys belonged to the American Bar Association, and only 42 per cent of the teachers to the National Education Association. Only 45 per cent of America's 344,823 doctors were reported to be dues-paying members of the American Medical Association in June, 1972, in *San Francisco Chronicle* (June 17, 1972), p. 5.

79. Wilbert E. Moore, "But Some Are More Equal Than Others," *American Sociological Review* 24 (February, 1963): 13–18.

80. See William A. Glaser, *Social Settings and Medical Organization: A Cross-National Study of the Hospital* (New York: Atherton Press, 1970); Eliot Freidson, ed., *The Hospital in Modern Society* (New York: The Free Press, 1963); Charles Perrow, "Hospitals: Technology, Structure, and Goals," in James G. March, ed., *Handbook of Organizations* (Chicago: Rand McNally & Company, 1965), pp. 910–71.

81. Cynthia F. Epstein, "Encountering the Male Establishment: Sex-Status Limits on Women's Careers in the Professions," *American Journal of Sociology* 75 (May, 1970): 968–82, at 981.

82. Wilbert E. Moore, *The Professions: Roles and Rules* (New York: Russell Sage Foundation, 1970), p. 167.

83. Hughes, "License and Mandate," in *Men and Their Work,* p. 79.

84. Goode, "Theoretical Limits," in Etzioni, ed., *The Semi-Professions and Their Organization,* p. 291.

85. Moore, *Professions,* p. 112.

86. Hughes, "License and Mandate," pp. 69–70.

87. For some of the problems involved, see Michael Lipsky, "Toward a Theory of Street-Level Bureaucracy," in Michael W. Kirst, *State, School, and Politics* (Lexington, Mass.: D. C. Heath and Company, 1972), pp. 205–12.

88. William J. Goode, "Community within Community: The Professions," *American Sociological Review* 22 (April, 1967): 194–200.

89. Marshall, *Class, Citizenship,* p. 165, has argued that the professions "have not always struck a true balance between loyalty to the client and loyalty to the community, and they have sometimes treated loyalty to the profession as an end rather than as a means to the fulfillment of other loyalties. They are often accused of neglecting the public welfare."

90. Parsons, "The Professions," p. 36: "Perhaps even it is not mainly a difference of typical motives at all, but one of the different situations in which much the same commonly human motives operate. Perhaps the acquisitiveness of modern business is institutional rather than motivational."

91. Gilb, *Hidden Hierarchies;* David B. Truman, *The Governmental Process: Political Interests and Public Opinion,* 2nd ed. (New York: Alfred A. Knopf, 1971), pp. 93–98, 168–69, 249–50, 452–53.

92. These investigations were made possible in part by a training grant from the National Institute of Mental Health, in part by support for dissertation research from the National Science Foundation, and in part by fellowship support from the Social Science Research Council, the Danforth Foundation, and the Mabelle McLeod Lewis Research Fund.

93. Harold E. Quinley, *The Prophetic Clergy: Social Activism among Protestant Ministers* (New York: John Wiley, 1974).

94. J. Vincent Buck, "City Planners: The Dilemma of Professionals in a Political Milieu" (Ph.D. diss., Stanford University, 1972).

95. Philip R. Lochner, Jr., "Learning to be a Lawyer: Homogenization and Differentiation into Public and Private Sector Professional Roles" (Ph.D. diss., Stanford University, 1971).

96. Ruth Ann Becker, "Potential Groups: An Exploration of the Conditions and Processes of Group Formation among Doctors and Lawyers (Ph.D. diss., Stanford University, 1975).

97. Robert O'Connor, "Scientists in Politics: A Study in Political Participation" (Ph.D. diss., Stanford University, 1974).

98. Edie Goldenberg, *Making the Papers: The Access of Resource-Poor Groups to the Metropolitan Press* (Lexington, Mass.: D. C. Heath, 1975).

99. Ellen B. Levine, "Role Conflicts among Black Businessmen" (Ph.D. diss., Stanford University, 1974).

100. See Glendon Schubert, *The Public Interest* (Glencoe: The Free Press, 1960), p. 11: "Most of the literature characteristically tends either to define the public interest as a universal, in terms so broad that it encompasses almost any type of specific decision, or else to particularize the concept, by identifying with the most specific and discrete of policy norms and actions, to the extent that it has no general significance."

101. Michael Harrington, *The Other America* (New York: The Macmillan Company, 1962).

102. See Herbert Kaufman, "Administrative Decentralization and Political Power," *Public Administration Review* 29 (January-February, 1969): 3−14.

103. Marshall, *Class, Citizenship,* p. 164.

104. See Michael Lipsky, "Protest as a Political Resource," *American Political Science Review* 62 (December 1968): 1144−58; James Q. Wilson, "The Strategy of Protest: Problems of Negro Civic Action," *Journal of Conflict Resolution* 3 (September, 1961): 290−303.

105. See Bertram M. Beck, "Community Control: A Distraction, Not an Answer," *Social Work* 14 (October, 1969): 14−20. For an opposite point of view, see Marilyn Gittell, "Professionalism and Public Participation in Educational Policy Making: New York City, A Case Study," *Public Administration Review* 27 (September, 1967): 237−51. See also Henry M. Levin, ed., *Community Control of Schools* (Washington, D.C.: The Brookings Institution, 1970).

106. Moore, *Professions,* p. 169. See Theodore J. Lowi, *The Politics of Disorder* (New York: Basic Books, 1971), p. 80: "Decentralization through delegation of power merely meant conversion from government control to a far more irresponsible, enigmatic, unpredictable group control."

107. Hughes, "License and Mandate," p. 54. As Hughes continues, the professional's "very competence comes from having dealt with a thousand cases of what the client likes to consider his unique trouble."

108. Marie R. Haug and Marvin B. Sussman, "Professional Autonomy and the Revolt of the Client," *Social Problems* 17 (Fall, 1969): p. 156.

109. Alexander M. Carr-Saunders, "Metropolitan Conditions and Traditional Professional Relationships," in Robert M. Fisher, ed., *The Metropolis in Modern Life* (Garden City, N.Y.: Doubleday and Company, 1955), p. 283, writes: "As a consequence of the trend toward specialization, the professional man no longer takes a comprehensive interest in his client. He feels that he has no general responsibility for those who come under his care, and the personal relationship between practitioner and client is weakened."

110. See Helen Merrell Lynd, *On Shame and the Search for Identity,* (New York: Science Editions, 1965).

111. Haug and Sussman, "Professional Autonomy," pp. 157−58.

112. Ibid., p. 159.

113. Ibid., p. 160.

114. Michael Lipsky, *Protest in City Politics: Rent Strikes, Housing and the Power of the Poor* (Chicago: Rand McNally & Company, 1970), p. 168.

115. See Michael G. Michaelson, "Medical Students: Healers Become Activists," *Saturday*

Review (August 16, 1969): 41−43, 53−54; Robert J. Bazell, "Health Radicals: Crusade to Shift Medical Power to the People," *Science* 173 (August 6, 1971): 506−09.

116. George A. Brager, "Advocacy and Political Behavior," *Social Work* 13 (April, 1968): 5−15, at 15.

117. Richard Du Cann, *The Art of the Advocate* (London: Penguin Books, 1964).

118. Schein, *Professional Education*, p. 51.

119. See Martin Meyerson and Edward C. Banfield, *Politics, Planning, and the Public Interest* (Glencoe: The Free Press, 1955); Alan Altshuler, *The City Planning Process: A Political Analysis* (Ithaca, N.Y.: Cornell University Press, 1965); Francine F. Rabinovitz, *City Politics and Planning* (New York: Atherton Press, 1969).

120. This was recognized in an early study by Peter H. Rossi and Robert A. Dentler, *The Politics of Urban Renewal* (Glencoe: The Free Press, 1961).

121. See Earl M. Blecher, *Advocacy Planning for Urban Development: With Analysis of Six Demonstration Programs* (New York: Praeger Publishers, 1971).

122. Marks, *The Lawyer, the Public*, p. 250.

123. Gilb, *Hidden Hierarchies*, p. 89.

124. Client control, however, may be frustrated by what Clark Kerr calls "institutional markets" in which the boundaries of service are not set by the participants in the consultative relationship but by institutional rules. See Clark Kerr, "The Balkanization of Labor Markets," in E. Wight Bakke et al., eds., *Labor Mobility and Economic Opportunity* (New York: John Wiley & Sons, 1954), p. 93.

125. Multiple advocacy as a conscious decision-making strategy is recommended by Alexander L. George, "The Case for Multiple Advocacy in Making Foreign Policy," *American Political Science Review* 66 (September, 1972): 751−85.

126. Rourke, *Bureaucracy*, p. 45.

127. See Donald C. Pelz, "Interaction and Attitudes between Scientists and the Auxiliary Staff," *Administrative Science Quarterly* 4 (December, 1959): 321−36, and 4 (March, 1960): 410−25.

128. Gilb, *Hidden Hierarchies*, pp. 162−64.

129. Moore, *The Professions*, p. 73.

130. "There are professional ethics for the priest, the soldier, the lawyer, the magistrate, and so on," Durkheim observed three quarters of a century ago, and then asked: "Why should there not be one for trade and industry?" Emile Durkheim, *Professional Ethics and Civic Morals* (Glencoe: The Free Press, 1958), pp. 29−30. No answer has yet been forthcoming, but see Bernard Barber, "Is American Business Becoming Professionalized?" in Tiryakian, ed., *Sociological Theory, Values and Sociocultural Change*, pp. 121−45. The English Socialist R. H. Tawney argued, in *The Acquisitive Society* (New York: Harcourt, Brace and Company, 1920), chap. 7, "Industry as a Profession," that nationalization of industry was a necessary condition of its professionalization.

131. Daniel Bell comes to the same conclusion, if by a different route: "It is more likely, however, that the post-industrial society will involve *more* politics than ever before for the very reason that choice becomes conscious and the decision-centers more visible." See his essay, "The Measurement of Knowledge and Technology," in Eleanor B. Sheldon and Wilbert E. Moore, eds., *Indicators of Social Change: Concepts and Measurements* (New York: Russell Sage Foundation, 1968), p. 238.

132. On contemporary institutional trends, see Thomas E. Cronin and Sanford D. Greenberg, eds., *The Presidential Advisory System* (New York: Harper and Row, 1969); Committee on the Utilization of Young Scientists and Engineers in Advisory Services to Government, Office of Scientific Personnel, National Research Council, *The Science Committee*, 2 vols., (Washington, D.C.: National Academy of Sciences, 1972); Daniel Patrick Moynihan, "The Professionalization of Reform," *The Public Interest* 1 (Fall, 1965); 6−16; Advisory Committee on Government Programs in the Behavioral Sciences, National Research Council, *The Behavioral Sciences and the Federal Government* (Washington, D.C.: National Academy of Sciences, 1968); Special Commission on the Social Sciences of the National Science Board, *Knowledge into Action: Improving the Nation's Use of the Social Sciences* (Washington, D.C.: National Science Foundation, 1969).

INDEX